ALONG THE E&N

GLEN A. MOFFORD

A JOURNEY BACK TO
THE HISTORIC HOTELS
OF VANCOUVER ISLAND

TOUCHWOOD

Editing by Lana Okerlund
Design by Colin Parks
Cover image: The Strathcona Hotel at Shawnigan Lake; photo taken by Frank Burrell; image 2010-010-139 courtesy of the Oak Bay Archives

LIBRARY AND ARCHIVES CANADA CATALOGUING IN PUBLICATION

Title: Along the E&N : a journey back to the historic hotels of Vancouver Island / Glen Mofford.
Names: Mofford, Glen, 1954- author.
Description: Includes index.
Identifiers: Canadiana (print) 20190057238 | Canadiana (ebook) 20190057416 | ISBN 9781771512879 | (softcover) | ISBN 9781771512886 (PDF)
Subjects: LCSH: Historic hotels—British Columbia—Vancouver Island. | LCSH: Hotels—British Columbia—Vancouver Island. | LCSH: Vancouver Island (B.C.)—History.
Classification: LCC FC3844.7.H68 M64 2019 | DDC 971.1/2—dc23

We acknowledge the financial support of the Government of Canada through the Canada Book Fund and the Province of British Columbia through the Book Publishing Tax Credit.

The interior pages of this book have been printed on 100% post-consumer recycled paper, processed chlorine free, and printed with vegetable-based inks.

The information in this book is true and complete to the best of the author's knowledge. All recommendations are made without guarantee on the part of the author. The author disclaims any liability in connection with the use of this information.

PRINTED IN CANADA AT FRIESENS

23 22 21 20 19   1 2 3 4 5

IN MEMORY OF MY BIG BROTHER,
ROBERT (BOB) MOFFORD

CONTENTS

I HAVE A CONFESSION TO make. In 1968, I had a picture of a naked Pierre Berton hanging on my bedroom wall. While most teenagers had posters of buxom blondes, rock stars, or sports figures, I chose a popular Canadian journalist and historian to hang on my wall. There he was for all to see, Pierre Berton, sans clothing, set between my black-light posters, clippings of the Beatles, *Newsweek* and *Time* photographs of the Vietnam War, and a picture of the other Pierre smiling back at me during the height of Trudeaumania.

Let me explain.

The walls of my bedroom were strewn with the faces of my contemporary heroes, people I respected and admired. An artist's rendition of Pierre Berton was clipped from a copy of the *Star Weekly*, a supplement to the *Toronto Star.* Peter Gzowski was the new editor, and he took a staid and stale, money-losing newspaper and transformed it into arguably the finest weekly in the nation. Gzowski hammered out a deal with McClelland & Stewart, publishers of Berton's new book, *The Smug Minority*, for the *Star Weekly* to run a series of excerpts from the book. To publicize it, Gzowski hired Vancouver artist Roy Peterson to draw a large poster of Berton posing nude in the manner of Rodin's *Thinker*.[1] *Time Canada* "liked the sauciness of the magazine, especially the cartoon of Pierre Berton posing in psychedelic colour."[2] At the time, Berton was at the height of his popularity and the apex of his writing career. I spent countless hours far, far away in the goldfields

1

of the Klondike, or driving in a spike along the transcontinental railway, or defending Canada against American aggression during the War of 1812. I got lost in Canadian history, and it was Pierre Berton who provided the time machine.

Today that love for and fascination with Canadian history is as strong as ever, but now my walls are adorned with prints of artwork by Emily Carr, E.J. Hughes, Tom Thomson, and the Group of Seven. As I grew up, I developed my own path by researching and writing about people and places in British Columbia. Specifically, I discovered that I enjoy social history, especially when it pertains to historic hotels, from the proprietors who ran them to the characters who stayed there.

I have become particularly fascinated by the development of Vancouver Island hotels through the years. Some of the most amazing hotel entrepreneurs were responsible for founding towns that have grown into the thriving cities we see today on the island: remarkable pioneers like Swedish brothers Charles and Fred Thulin, who built the Willows Hotel in 1904, and by doing so put Campbell River on the map; or the ebullient retired brigadier general Noel Money, who built the Qualicum Beach Hotel and thereby contributed to the growth of that attractive resort community; or visionaries like Charles Morton, who repurposed a private residence at Shawnigan Lake and opened the first hotel in the area. And the list goes on of men and women who carved new communities out of wilderness from Esquimalt to Forbes Landing.

I've wanted to write a book about the historic hotels of Vancouver Island for years. Initially it was going to encompass the whole island, from Victoria to Cape Scott, but that would have involved over a hundred hotels, which I realized was far too ambitious (and the fact is, I have only a limited time on this earth), so I eventually got the number down to a manageable thirty-two hotels that once thrived along a carpet of wooden ties and steel rails called the Esquimalt and Nanaimo (E&N) Railway.

The long-term lease of the land to the E&N was a very generous one—twenty miles either side of the line from Victoria in the south to Campbell River in the north added up to approximately two million acres. Any existing homestead properties within the grant were excluded, but an extension of land was given to make up for those exempt properties.[3]

Just as the transcontinental railway linked Canada from east to west, the E&N Railway linked Vancouver Island south to north, playing a significant role in opening up parts of the island that had previously been inaccessible except to the many Indigenous peoples and the few explorers and prospectors who travelled over worn paths laid out through the ages. Isolated towns that hugged the east coast of Vancouver Island and relied solely on ships for supplies and news from the outside world now had the railroad as an alternative for transporting goods in and out of their communities. The few roads that existed in 1886 were crude and hazardous, and it would be years before they were improved with the advent of the automobile. In the meantime, the railroad filled the gap, breaking the isolation of many communities and allowing them to grow and prosper.[4] And as the communities expanded, existing businesses benefited, and new businesses emerged, including a variety of hotels, from luxurious resorts to the most modest inns.

I want to take you back in time as a passenger on one of the first E&N steam trains that rolled along the tracks of Vancouver Island. The geographic area we'll cover on our journey extends from Esquimalt to Courtenay, plus the subdivisions of Cowichan Bay, Lake Cowichan, Alberni, Great Central Lake, Cumberland, and Comox. Plans to extend the E&N to Campbell River and beyond came to an immediate halt with the outbreak of the First World War, so we are forced to take a bus to Campbell River and end at Forbes Landing. We will travel over hair-raising trestles that traverse creeks and rivers and climb mountains on the way to each community along the route. We will take in magnificent scenery, such as the farmlands of the Cowichan Valley and the pleasant shoreline from just north of Nanaimo to the Comox Valley.

Only nine of the featured hotels survive today, as neighbourhood pubs, but while researching this book, I found a treasure trove of material about their heydays. Stories abound about the history and character of many of the proprietors, owners, and visitors who lived at these pioneer hotels, and fading sepia photographs provide a window into their past. There were many more establishments I could have included, like the Wheatsheaf, the Fanny Bay, the Elk Hotel, and notable others, but the thirty-two I chose each have a long and fascinating story and reflect the unique history of their communities.

I hope the stories you're about to read bring back some happy memories for those lucky enough to have ridden up and down the island along the E&N and that they'll give those who missed that experience a second chance to ride those rails into the past. You've bought your ticket, so sit back and relax as we visit the historic hotels along the E&N. All aboard!

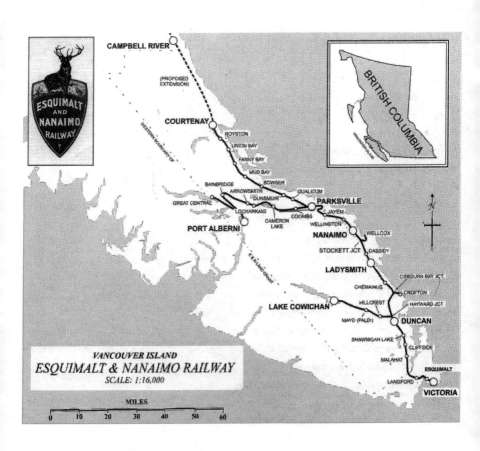

Above: Map of Vancouver Island depicting route of the E&N Railway.

ESQUIMALT DISTRICT

MILE 06

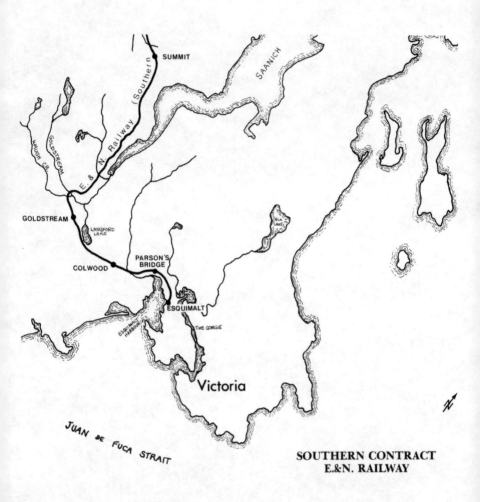

Above: Map of the southern stage of the E&N Railway, from Donald F. MacLachlan's
book *The Esquimalt & Nanaimo Railway: The Dunsmuir Years: 1884–1905.*

CHAPTER 1

Esquimalt District

ALTHOUGH THE ESQUIMALT DISTRICT IS the oldest of all
the districts we will visit in this book, it wasn't incorporated until
September 1, 1912. Before the arrival of Europeans, the Indigenous
Coast Salish peoples had been living here for four thousand years.[1]
In 1848, Sir James Douglas negotiated a treaty with the local First
Nations, purchasing land for the Puget Sound Agricultural Company,
which split the land into three major farms. The Royal Navy took
advantage of the deep-sea harbour at Esquimalt and established its
main Pacific Fleet there in 1854. By then a small community had
been built in what is now Naden on Department of Defence lands,
and it grew from there. I have a personal interest in the community;
one hundred years after the Royal Navy established its base there,
my family lived in Esquimalt when I was born in 1954—a navy brat.

Robert Dunsmuir, with backing from three railway financiers,
signed an agreement with the federal government in 1883 to construct the E&N.[2] He had come a long way from his beginnings as
a coal miner working for the Hudson's Bay Company in 1850 to
a coal magnate by 1884. Esquimalt was also the starting point for
the southern crew of the E&N Railway, who worked north and
eventually joined up with the crew working south from Nanaimo.
The first survey for the E&N, Division 1, began in Esquimalt near
Plumper Bay, opposite Inskip Island on the Songhees Reserve, on

May 7, 1884. The Division 2 survey team started in Nanaimo on May 16, 1884, working south.[3] In early 1885, construction of the E&N began simultaneously in Nanaimo and Esquimalt. The two teams would join up on August 13, 1886, near Shawnigan Lake, just south of Strathcona Lodge, at a place called Cliffside, where Prime Minister Sir John A. Macdonald drove in the last spike that signified the completion of the first phase of the E&N. A number of extensions would follow over the next few years. The first extension off the main line was built from Thetis Cove in Esquimalt south to Russell's Station (near Lime Bay, where Spinnakers Brew Pub and Guesthouses is located today)[4] and then across the new swing bridge to Victoria (completed in March 1888).[5] And right near Russell's Station is our first stop: the Halfway House.

HALFWAY HOUSE

1860 – 2017

The Halfway House[6] predated the E&N by twenty-six years and outlasted the life of the railway, closing without much fanfare or warning on October 22, 2017, as the Cambie at Esquimalt Pub. Located along the 800 block of Esquimalt Road, the modest building that housed both pub and liquor store may have appeared rather ordinary, and its closing did not receive much coverage in the press, but its worn exterior masked a remarkable 157-year history.

On this site in 1860, when Esquimalt Road was a dirt trail and Victoria was two years away from incorporation, a small hotel and tavern opened to the public. The Halfway House, as it was initially named, was the oldest private business operating from its original location by the time it shut its doors as the Cambie. This old hostelry deserves a book of its own, but I have elected to tell the story of its earliest years, from 1860 to 1892.

Facing page: Elizabeth and James William Bland opened the Halfway House in 1860. It was Esquimalt's oldest privately operated business when it closed in 2016. Image G01333 courtesy of the Royal BC Museum and Archives.

On February 3, 1859, James William and Elizabeth Bland arrived in Victoria after a long voyage from England. The following year, they purchased a large property in Esquimalt, where they built their home and a tavern that they named the Halfway House. While building their new home, they stayed at Constant Cove in a house owned by sawmill magnate Edward Stamp.[7]

Offering a barroom as well as "comfortable rooms, clean stables and wholesome food for sailors and settlers,"[8] the new tavern became a popular stop as the halfway point on the trail between the town of Victoria and the British naval base at Esquimalt Harbour. Patrons enjoyed the unique beer that James Bland brewed from water drawn at three wells on the property. Bland registered his brewery in 1861, and "his recipe was used by family members for years. One of his secrets was the use of Muscat raisins."[9]

On April 14, 1862, the steamer *Hermann* arrived at the Esquimalt docks from San Francisco and unloaded a most unusual cargo, twenty-three Bactrian camels, which caused quite a commotion in the small community and frightened the horses.[10] The two-humped animals were shedding their winter coats and did not look or smell very appealing. The camels were corralled on two acres of fenced land on the Bland property behind the Halfway House brewery until they were sold as pack animals for the Fraser River goldfields. It was also reported that the animals were guarded by a "live Turk."[11] People were naturally curious to view these strange and exotic beasts of burden, and Bland quickly recognized the advantage to his business that advertising them would bring. Onlookers were not disappointed and were especially delighted to witness the birth of a baby camel some days later.[12]

Over the next seventeen years, Elizabeth Bland gave birth to two children at the Halfway House, which brought the number of their brood up to five. During this period, James Bland attempted to sell the property and business at least twice, in November 1875 and again in July 1877. "That splendid property known as the Halfway House, situated on the Esquimalt Road, comprising two acres of arable land well-fenced, with three wells of the finest water on the premises," read one of the advertisements James ran to promote the sale. "The Building is substantially built of Brick, with all necessary Outbuildings, etc. A first-class Brewery is attached with every article for Brewing; the Boiler has a capacity of 200 gallons at a Brewing. There is also a capital Skittle or Bowling Alley on the premises."[13] These efforts were to no avail, however.

Perhaps the Blands were getting tired of it all. Late one evening, for instance, when the Blands had closed for business and retired to bed, they heard some shouting outside their window. James looked down on three sailors and noticed that they appeared to have had enough grog for one night. They asked if they could buy some beer and, after being informed that the tavern was closed, refused take no for an answer. Fed up and not in the mood to argue, James proceeded to dump the contents of a full chamber pot onto the heads of the unsuspecting sailors and repeated that the bar was closed.[14]

The Blands eventually did sell their property and business, in 1888, but not before one dramatic moment that could have resulted in disaster. In January that year, a fire broke out in the Halfway House and threatened to consume the business and the house. Quick action by the local fire brigade saved both structures. Fire was the single greatest cause of destruction in Greater Victoria at the time and remained so for many years.

On May 17, 1888, the new owner, Joseph Bayley, late of the Occidental Hotel in Victoria, took over the business and began the first of what would be numerous renovations to the tavern over the years. He built a brick addition to the original wood building and named it the Trentham Hotel. He improved the bowling green and turned the original building into a restaurant. Over time, the brick addition would become the main building, and a second floor was added in 1925 to satisfy liquor board regulations that required a minimum of rooms in order to be granted a liquor licence.

Bayley operated the hotel for a few shaky years until his mental health came into question. Apparently, he enjoyed drinking to excess, which usually got him in trouble. In November 1891, Bayley, "crazed with drink," and perhaps distraught over the prospect of having to sell his hotel and property, was arrested for disturbing the peace and ended up in the Victoria jail at Bastion Square.[15] "Joseph Bayley, the semi-demented proprietor of the Halfway House is still in custody on a charge of insanity," the *Daily Colonist* reported.[16] The court determined that Bayley was sane, and a deal was worked out in which Bayley signed over the hotel and property to his wife. In May 1892, the Trentham Hotel was sold at auction, allowing Bayley to retire back to the old country.

The above stories are but a very brief peek into the history of this landmark establishment. I recall so many memories of the place from when I occasionally popped in for a drink during its last few decades of business—the great pub food in the 1960s through '80s; line dancing and live country music; watching my friend Geoff have the dubious honour of being the first person arrested under a new smoking bylaw back in January 1999.[17] But those stories are for another time.

Passengers holding tickets on the E&N may have stopped in at the Trentham Hotel for lunch and a quick drink before boarding the train at Russell's Station on their way up island. It was a short train ride from there to Esquimalt Station near Thetis Bay on the View Royal and Esquimalt border. Once out of that station, the train crossed the old dirt Colwood Road (which would eventually become the Old Island Highway), just a stone's throw from the Four Mile House.

The Four Mile House when it operated briefly as a tea house offering midnight dinners in 1941. Image M00464 courtesy of the City of Victoria Archives.

FOUR MILE HOUSE

SINCE 1858

Two popular roadhouses in the Esquimalt District were in business for many years before the E&N came along in 1886: the Four Mile House (licensed in 1864) and the Parson's Bridge Hotel (licensed in 1856, the oldest licensed establishment in British Columbia), later known as the Six Mile House. Both were linked to Fort Victoria, approximately four to six miles away, by the Colwood Road, and it took a horse and buggy a full day to travel to these establishments—and that was on days when the weather cooperated. It took much longer and was certainly less comfortable in inclement conditions. The arrival of the E&N made it much easier to travel between Victoria and the western farming communities than ever before, and that translated to more regular paying customers for each of the roadhouses and the means to expand and improve their businesses.

The Four Mile House was built in 1858 on the six acres of land where Caleb Pike and his bride of two years (she married at the age of sixteen), Elizabeth (née Lidgate), resided. Their Craigflower property extended from both sides of the Colwood Road and sloped down to Esquimalt Harbour. The couple had their share of tragedies: a baby boy, Robert, lived less than a week, and a daughter, Helen (or Ellen), was born in December 1858 but died in August 1860.[18]

In July 1864, Caleb Pike was granted a country liquor licence. This is the earliest evidence that the Pikes ran a roadhouse and sold beer and spirits near Craigflower.[19] The initial name of the tavern is unknown, but in the 1865 revised assessment is the name Four Mile House. Caleb and Elizabeth ran the roadhouse until at least 1867, when they decided to sell and move to Yew Tree Farm in the Highland District. The new owners of the Four Mile House were Peter and Elizabeth Calvert.

The Calverts arrived in the Craigflower area in the early 1860s. Peter Calvert worked in the Steamboat Exchange Saloon, which opened in Esquimalt in August 1863, until they purchased the Four Mile House. At first using Four Mile as their private residence, over time they began serving food and tending the horses of the travellers who rested there from their long journey along the Colwood Road that connected Victoria to the farms in the west. Elizabeth cooked while Peter looked after the animals. Elizabeth spoke Chinook fluently and employed an Indigenous couple, Joe and "Shrimpy," whose duties included washing and keeping the new inn supplied with the fresh shrimp and crab that was in great demand at the time.[20]

Perhaps the Calverts just wanted a change, but by the summer of 1872, they leased the Parson's Bridge Hotel (later known as the Six Mile House). They continued to own the Four Mile House but leased it out to business partners Augustus and Clark.[21] All was well for a few years as both businesses flourished, but the summer of 1877 brought tragedy.

On a pleasant warm day in July 1877, a picnic was under way when Peter Calvert went to fetch some water from a nearby spring using his horses and buggy. On the way, the shaft of the buggy broke and fell on the heels of the horses, spooking them into an immediate gallop. A surprised Calvert hung on to the buggy and attempted to calm the horses, but before he could rein them in and gain control, the runaway carriage hit a tree stump, sending Calvert ten feet into the air. Landing head first on the hard ground, he was knocked unconscious while the terrified horses continued on, dragging the empty buggy behind them. Mr. Winter, who had been riding close behind and saw the horrific accident, was the first to render aid to the motionless Calvert. Dr. Redgrave also soon arrived to attend to the stricken man and, with the aid of friends at the picnic, managed to get Calvert home.[22] He remained in a coma for six days before succumbing to his injuries on the afternoon of July 25, 1877.

After the death of her husband, Elizabeth Calvert returned to the Four Mile House and had the hotel refurbished, reopening it in 1878. That summer was a productive one for Mrs. Calvert and her hotel. The steamer *Leonora* began afternoon excursion trips from the Hudson's Bay wharf in Victoria Harbour to the Esquimalt wharf, with stops at the Six Mile House and Four Mile House before returning to Victoria. The five-hour round-trip cost one dollar and proved to be a big hit with the public, who got to see the Royal Navy fleet inside Esquimalt Harbour in all its glory as well as enjoy lunch and a beverage at the two popular roadhouses.[23]

On one particularly cold winter evening in February 1879, a guest imbibing at the Four Mile House made the fateful decision to ride home in the ice and snow. Robert Kerr lived less than two miles from the roadhouse, but he never made it. He was found about one hundred yards from the front door of his home, dead from exposure.[24] Robert Kerr had arrived in Victoria in 1859 and served as attorney general in both British Crown colonies of Vancouver Island and British Columbia, and he was instrumental in having the capital of British Columbia moved from New Westminster to Victoria.[25]

At twenty-nine years of age, Elizabeth Calvert remarried, on December 10, 1879; her second husband was thirty-six-year-old William Calvert, Peter's younger brother.[26] But within five years, Elizabeth was widowed again when William died on March 28,

1884, after a lingering illness.[27] Elizabeth married for a third time, on September 3, 1885, this time to an American blacksmith, John Conway, who lived in Victoria. Elizabeth appears to have had the worst luck with men because, a few months after her third marriage, she almost lost her new husband to a chicken thief.

One winter evening a few days before Christmas, Conway was awoken by strange noises. Upon investigation, he noticed some movement in the chicken coop out back. He approached the coop and confronted a man attempting to steal some chickens. The thief turned, and that's when Conway noticed he was carrying a handgun. The two struggled for the pistol, and a shot rang out, harmlessly adding a new hole to the chicken coop roof. Conway eventually subdued the thief and held him until a police constable arrived. The constable immediately recognized the thief as Sing Lee, a notorious chicken thief who had only recently been discharged after serving a month in jail for attempting to steal chickens at the Colonist Hotel.[28] Lee was cuffed and carted off to jail while Elizabeth and John Conway breathed a sigh of relief after the ordeal.

There are so many more stories to tell about the very long and interesting history of Four Mile House. The building survives today in what is now the municipality of View Royal, although it has undergone countless renovations and modifications over the years. It still stood as one of the oldest buildings in Greater Victoria in 2018 and houses a popular and very successful brew pub and restaurant.

Our journey continues about two miles north along the E&N to the small station constructed behind Parson's Bridge Hotel in 1886 for the first passenger trains.

PARSON'S BRIDGE HOTEL (SIX MILE HOUSE)
SINCE 1855

Many hotel and pub owners have claimed through the years that their establishment holds the oldest liquor licence in British

Six Mile House, ca. 1930s. Image M07743 courtesy of the City of Victoria Archives.

Columbia, but David Wong, owner of the Six Mile House can make that claim stick. The Parson's Bridge Hotel, later named the Six Mile House, opened in 1855 when Hudson's Bay Company millwright and former London bobby William (Bill) Parsons purchased forty acres of land from his employer and subsequently built Parson's Bridge and the hotel to go with it.[29]

The hotel was set on a rocky ledge located on the eastern side of a rickety old bridge over Millstream Creek. The one-storey wooden building also had a veranda, and it was a welcome sight for farmers who lived beyond the Millstream and travelled by horse and buggy or wagon along the long, rough road to Victoria. Parsons's barroom was also popular with Royal Navy sailors who frequented the hotel when collecting fresh water from the Millstream or while on leave from the nearby Esquimalt naval base.

Shortly after opening his hotel and bar, Parsons ran into trouble with the authorities. Apparently, he was selling beer and liquor in his bar without the mandatory liquor licence. Parsons pleaded guilty and was ordered to pay a small fine, but the incident did not prejudice him from applying for and receiving a country liquor licence in 1856.

A two-storey addition with a balcony was attached to the east end of the original building, and eventually the older structure was replaced. From 1867 to 1870, Parson's Bridge Hotel was leased to Charles Berry Brown, an experienced hotelman who had run the Island Hotel on Government Street in Victoria in the early 1860s. While running the Parson's Bridge Hotel, Brown was forced to call the local constable when he caught an Indigenous man nicknamed "Cock Eye" in the act of stealing his silver watch and other valuables. The man pleaded guilty and was sentenced to two months' imprisonment with hard labour. Cock Eye had only recently been released off a chain-gang for an offence he had committed in Nanaimo.[30]

In 1872, Brown moved back to Victoria, where he opened Brown's Hotel on the corner of Fort and Douglas Streets. Taking over the lease for the Parson's Bridge Hotel were Peter and Elizabeth Calvert, who ran it from August 1872 until Peter's death on July 25, 1877 (see Four Mile House). That same year, the bridge across Millstream was condemned, jeopardizing the liquor licence for the hotel.[31] The bridge was eventually replaced.

In the 1880s, brothers Richard (Jim) and Henry Price became the new owners and operators of the Parson's Bridge Hotel, with Richard Graham as head bartender. A teamster during the exciting Cariboo gold rush, Henry Price ran the hotel until he was succeeded by his nephew.[32] It was during Price's tenure, sometime in 1898, that the name changed from the Parson's Bridge Hotel to the familiar Six Mile House.[33]

A number of E&N Railway accidents occurred near the hotel through the years. The most tragic took place on September 15, 1900, just north of Ladysmith, when engine no. 1 heading south collided with engine no. 10 heading north, killing four people.[34] Several years later, on November 4, 1905, at five-thirty PM, a southbound freight train of thirty cars derailed on the E&N line just above the Six Mile House. Sixteen of the cars came off the tracks, and many were totally destroyed. "The cars swayed and toppled over the bank in debris, sixteen of them piling up at the bottom of the embankment . . . it was believed the accident was caused by spreading rails . . . none of the train crew were injured."[35] While the derailment did not result in any deaths, there was concern that, despite the sale of the E&N to the new owners, the Canadian Pacific Railway (CPR) in 1905, accidents continued to take place all along the line.

Meanwhile, the day-to-day routine of running the Six Mile House continued—though the E&N accident was the main topic of conversation in the bar at the time. The bar continued to provide the bulk of the hotel's profit despite run-ins with some questionable liquor laws. For example, proprietor Jim Price was fined $100 in provincial police court because he did not have the barroom curtains drawn on a Sunday, as required by law.[36] On another occasion, Price found himself in court again, this time for serving an underage boy, sixteen-year-old F.H. Casey. Price was fined a hundred dollars for that offence as well. Casey must have had quite a drinking spree because the proprietors of the Gorge Hotel, the Four Mile House, and the Colwood Hotel were also fined for serving him—although Daniel Campbell, proprietor of the Colwood Hotel (our next stop), managed an acquittal in the matter.[37]

In 1917, Price came up with a plan to dam the Millstream and raise trout. The scheme appeared to be working until heavy rains washed away his dream when the swollen river destroyed the dam and the holding pens for the trout.

In October later that same year, Prohibition legally ended the sale of liquor, but some hotel owners kept their bars open and sold "near beer" and other products acceptable under the law. Years later, when renovations were taking place at the Six Mile House, a number of empty whisky bottles were found in the walls of the bar, no doubt hidden away from the prying eyes of the law.[38]

Proud of its long tradition as a hospitable stop on the road to and from Victoria, the Six Mile House is going stronger than ever to this day. It no longer operates as a hotel, but the pub offers guests excellent food and a wide choice of spirits, craft beers, and non-alcoholic beverages.

COLWOOD HOTEL
1879–2003

The Colwood area opened to European settlement in the 1850s when the first Parson's Bridge was built, allowing settlers a wagon road to the lands west of the Millstream. In 1879, Andrew (Andy) J. Bechtel and his wife, Rachel, arrived in the area and built the first Colwood Hotel, a modest two-storey wood structure. Bechtel had worked as a hotelman for most of his adult life, and his new hotel was an immediate success as local residents used the facility as a social hub for meetings, gatherings, and events such as dances and dinners. The bar also got a lot of use in those pioneer days.

When the E&N was built in 1886, it was a windfall for each hotel along the route, including the Colwood Hotel, located at the junction of Goldstream and Metchosin Roads. As a stop for the train, the Colwood profited from the arrival of carloads of potential customers.

From 1888 to 1897, the "no-nonsense" Bechtel leased the hotel out to manage and bartend at Victoria's notorious California Saloon on Johnson Street. Wearing his favourite "tasselled smoking cap . . . he delighted in tossing recalcitrant sailors into the street."[39] Meanwhile, Colwood manager William McNeill, formally of the provincial police, ramped up the hotel's advertising and organized events to attract customers. Picnics, shooting matches, and similar events took place in the summer, while skating parties proved a popular draw in the winter months.[40]

December 12, 1895, proved to be an unlucky day for the Colwood Hotel when the sixteen-year-old structure was destroyed

A second and larger Colwood Hotel replaced the original that burned down in December 1895. Image M01027 courtesy of the City of Victoria Archives.

by fire. While that fact was disturbing enough, it was later determined that the fire was started deliberately and that an incendiary device was used.[41] The building and its contents were estimated to be worth $4,000. Following the fire, Bechtel decided to rebuild, and the larger two-storey Colwood Hotel reopened in June 1896 under the direction of Frank Shier. Meanwhile, the Commercial Union Assurance Company offered a $200 reward for the apprehension and conviction of whomever was responsible for the fire.[42]

Six years after the new Colwood Hotel was built, another fire came close to destroying it too. On September 10, 1902, a controlled bush burn near the hotel got out of hand when strong winds blew the flames out of control. Employees of the Colwood Hotel rushed outside when the fire alarm sounded and began fighting the fire. Their efforts saved the hotel.[43]

In 1903, the Bechtels gave the Colwood Hotel to their sons, Andrew Albert Bechtel, who became managing director of the Victoria Machinery Depot, and Daniel Arthur Bechtel, a doctor at the time. The Bechtel brothers hired Percy G. Clark, late of Duncan, to manage the popular hotel. Clark proved up to the challenge of running the establishment. One Sunday afternoon in the summer of 1904, some off-duty soldiers were enjoying themselves in the hotel bar. A few of the men had had too much to drink, and after repeated warnings, the bartender cut them off from service and asked them to leave. While most complied and prepared to depart, a few in the group took exception to being cut off and began to argue. The bartender stayed firm and threatened to throw them out of the hotel, and the soldiers finally left.

At six PM, the bartender was closing up the bar when some of the soldiers returned and attempted to force their way back inside, breaking a few windows in the process. The bartender called out for help from Clark, who immediately ran to the defence of his employee, shouting out a warning to the soldiers that he had a gun and wouldn't hesitate to use it. Some of the soldiers hesitated, but one soldier, Richard Flannagan, kept on smashing at the bar door. Clark took aim and a single shot rang out. Flannagan slumped to the floor with a wound in his leg.[44] The inquest into the shooting concluded that Clark had a legitimate right to protect himself, his staff, and his property from Flannagan's actions while under the influence. The charges against Clark were dismissed.

In November 1905, Clark transferred the Colwood's liquor licence to a new proprietor, Daniel Campbell. A carpenter by trade, Campbell had a checkered past. In 1901, he had followed his Scottish-born stepfather, John Donald "Jock" Campbell, and joined the BC Provincial Police. Dan and his wife, Florence, had three children at the time, and Campbell found it difficult to make ends meet on his meagre monthly salary of sixty-five dollars. Although his salary rose to seventy dollars a month in 1905, it didn't alleviate the family's financial problems, and one day Campbell made a bad decision.

"On 29 August 1905, Campbell shook down two women for $30 after stopping them in a horse and buggy that appeared out of control.

The ladies gave officer Campbell an address of a hotel in a known red-light district where he took them then demanded $30 for their release."[45] When asked about this, Campbell stated that he had helped the two ladies recover their goods and calmed the horse down, then returned them safely to their hotel, where they had given him thirty dollars. After an inquiry, Campbell was dismissed on September 28, 1905, for conduct unbecoming a policeman, conduct injurious to the public service, and accepting money without approval. Two months later, he began managing the Colwood Hotel.

Initially, Campbell leased the Colwood from the Bechtel brothers, but in November 1908, his mother, Margaret Jane Campbell, bought the hotel from the Bechtels for $3,500. In 1913, Margaret passed the hotel on to her son and his wife, who had taken a mortgage out on the property.

The hotel did a brisk business, with the E&N train continuing to bring new customers to its doors. The special trains were particularly welcome, bringing people out from Victoria for evening skating parties and daytime hunting events, such as the Big Turkey Shoot held at the Colwood Hotel, to which participants were reminded to "bring your own rifles."[46]

When it came to their personal finances, however, the Campbells always seemed to struggle. In October 1917, a bad financial outlook grew grimmer as Prohibition ended the revenue stream coming from the popular hotel bar. In desperation, Campbell found additional income when he rejoined the police as a special (temporary) constable. One of his first duties was to assist the regular police force in tracking down and capturing draft dodgers in the Cumberland area. The police were told to search for one person in particular, a labour leader and well-known agitator, Albert "Ginger" Goodwin. Campbell carried his own rifle, a .30-30 calibre Marlin, and was reputed to be a crack shot.[47] On July 27, 1918, Campbell caught up with Goodwin on a trail at the confluence of Cruikshank River and Rees Creek near Comox Lake and Cumberland and shot Goodwin dead.[48]

In 1919, the Campbells were forced to sell the thirteen-room Colwood Hotel and the five acres of land it stood on. Harry and Grace Shaw purchased the property for $7,500.[49] The hotel changed hands again in 1923 when the Shaws sold it to Mary "Ma" Greening Miller-Smith. I'll give you the full details about Ma Miller when we arrive at our next destination, the Goldstream Hotel (later Inn), but suffice to say here that she operated the Colwood and oversaw the opening of its beer parlour before selling it in April 1930 to George T. Quincy for $15,000 in order to rebuild her Goldstream Inn, which had burned down in 1923.

By 1936, Quincy felt it was time to modernize the Colwood Hotel. Instead of renovating the existing building, however, Quincy decided to demolish the old landmark and erect a whole new structure. The 1895 hotel was torn down and replaced with a mock Tudor-style building that housed a number of rooms and a spacious modern beer parlour complete with separate entrances for men and women.[50]

The newly named Colwood Inn continued to operate for the next several decades under a number of different proprietors. Then, in 2000, partners Lee and Mike Spence, Brad Arnold, and Robin Murdock purchased the old hostelry and renamed it the Crossroads Bar and Grill, a family-friendly community gathering spot where everyone would be welcome. On March 31, 2012, the Crossroads closed, and the building was raised off its foundations, cut into sections, and removed to another location to make way for the Capital City Centre development. It was sad to witness this historic building, with hundreds of stories to tell, sitting dark, empty, and boarded up, just rotting away. Calls to find a new owner for the structure went unanswered, so on December 21, 2017, the once proud Colwood Hotel building was demolished.[51]

THE GOLDSTREAM HOUSE

JAMES PHAIR, PROPRIETOR.

This commodious and well appointed House, situated at Goldstream, about eleven miles from Victoria, is the terminus for pleasure seekers of one of the most beautiful drives in British Columbia.

Picturesque Surroundings. Excellent Trout Fishing. A First-class Hotel.

THE IDEAL SPOT FOR A SUNDAY VISIT.

Goldstream Hotel, Vancouver Island, B.C.

Left: Advertisement for the original Goldstream Hotel, ca. 1887. Author's collection.

Above: Postcard of the Goldstream Hotel, ca. 1906. Author's collection.

GOLDSTREAM HOTEL (MA MILLER'S)

SINCE 1880

Goldstream Trail was the name given by white settlers to the footpath that branched north off the Metchosin Road and wound its way through the woods. The trail was made by Indigenous people and used for hundreds of years before the arrival of the Hudson's Bay Company, which began farming this area north from Victoria. The footpath then became a horse trail and, as more settlers came, a rough road wide enough to accommodate wagons and buggies. Goldstream got its name from the discovery of traces of gold in the 1860s. On October 24, 1863, a special licensing court granted four groups mining licences to dig at Goldstream.[52] The following April, interest in the Goldstream quartz mines saw up to a hundred men working for various companies searching for gold in the district. The representatives asked the government for funds to "complete a road through to the mines" in order for them to move in the equipment necessary to do their job.[53]

In July 1864, Hy Hibblethwaite, a shareholder in one of the gold-mining interests in the area, opened the St. Nicholas Hotel. The roadside hotel was a welcome sight for the growing number of farmers who travelled long distances to market their goods and get supplies from Victoria. Farms were miles apart, and the hotel was a place where neighbours could meet over a good meal or a drink. Hibblethwaite went into partnership with Charles Ashe, and they enlarged the business in March 1865.[54] Ashe seemed to have a difficult time adjusting to his new surroundings, however. He reported in May 1868 that some of his possessions were stolen and that, while he searched for them on Burnside Road, "some miscreant in human shape" had shot his horse out from under him.[55]

By 1870, a regular stage ran between Victoria and the Goldstream district. "A conveyance will leave James Mady's Market Exchange (on Fort Street) every Sunday morning at 8 o'clock calling at James Strachan's Wharf Street (Ship Inn), and returning will leave Goldstream at 4 o'clock."[56] James Mady (along with Peterson) also owned the Goldstream House, with "meals served at all hours with all liquors and wines mixed at the bar," according to an October 1870 newspaper ad. The following year, Mady's Market Exchange in Victoria was renamed the Royal Hotel.

An early ad for the Goldstream House from July 30, 1880, mentions that "it is charmingly situated on the bank of the Goldstream, a delightful ten-mile drive from Victoria. How can anyone not be lured to their hotel after reading the following: 'Pure Goldstream water is supplied free of charge. This water smooths the wrinkles of old age, gives health to the sick, beauty to the young and wisdom to all.'"[57]

This original Goldstream House must have been open for only a few seasons, as nothing further appears about a hotel by this name until February 1887, when a call for tenders to erect a two-storey hotel at Goldstream was announced in the *Daily Colonist*.[58]

This new hotel was designed by architect Elmer H. Fisher, who had also designed a number of other buildings on the West Coast, including the Alhambra Hotel in the Byrnes Block at Granville (Gastown) in Vancouver.[59] Proprietor James Phair paid approximately $7,000 to complete the new hotel, which was now connected to the E&N Railway just steps away. Phair was also the postmaster for the Goldstream area, and he would exchange the mail bags when the train stopped briefly at the trackside station.

The E&N was affordable, giving people with modest means the freedom to travel to destinations previously closed to them. The hotels put on weekend events, and the E&N provided special trains to get people there and home again. For a mere twenty-five cents, one could enjoy concerts, picnics, and swimming in the summer and skating in the winter, plus lunch at either the Colwood or Goldstream hotel. These events grew in popularity, and the hotels and the E&N did a brisk business. The Sunday concerts were especially well attended and were extended into other days of the week.[60]

Phair spent money on advertising his new hotel, and he worked out agreements with the E&N to bring guests to the Goldstream on special excursion trains. He allowed the militia to use a clearing on his lands as a firing range, "ensuring more thirsty customers in the saloon after rifle practice."[61] Phair also built a series of trails that allowed guests to get out and enjoy nature. The trails eventually led down to the river in what is now Goldstream campground.

In October 1906, the Goldstream Hotel and the land it stood on, which was just shy of a hundred acres, went up for sale, and in December, Phair auctioned off his cattle, horses, sheep, goats, pigs, farm implements, tools, hay, oats, and more—also serving a scrumptious lunch to those attending the action. But it wasn't until 1909 that Phair sold the land and Goldstream Hotel to Charles E. Pooley.

Arriving in British Columbia from England in 1862, Pooley had been fairly successful prospecting for gold during the Cariboo gold rush, and he had subsequently studied to be a lawyer, spending twelve years travelling British Columbia with Judge Matthew B. Begbie as registrar of the Supreme Court.[62] He didn't stay in the hotel business for very long, though. In April 1910, Pooley sold the hotel and thirty-three acres of land to William and Mary Miller of

Vancouver for $15,000. (Although Pooley kept most of the land for farming, he didn't have long to enjoy it; he died in March 1912.)

The Millers immediately began improvements to the hotel and grounds once the sale was finalized.[63] Mr. Miller was a career hotelier, having grown up in the business in Montreal. He had come to British Columbia to try his luck in the goldfields during the Klondike rush but found that running a hotel was his specialty. He moved to Vancouver around 1905, then to Vancouver Island to purchase the Goldstream Hotel.[64]

The Millers' renovation of the Goldstream Hotel brought it up to date. The hotel was an attractive and comfortable resort set in beautiful Goldstream, where the leaves of the trees turned all colours in the fall and where the summer sun shone down on trainloads of day trippers who came to enjoy a walk on one of the many trails or a game on the hotel grounds, or simply to rest by the gurgling stream.

This peaceful setting was upset on July 5, 1915, when tragedy struck. Mr. Miller and three friends were returning from Shawnigan Lake when their car went off the road at the mile 19 curve on the Malahat. Miller was "hurled through the air to the sloping hard ground below falling upon a rocky portion of the hillside and then being crushed beneath the heavy car."[65] There were no seatbelts in those days, and it was a miracle that the other three occupants, who had also been thrown from the automobile, survived with only minor scrapes and bruises.

Mrs. May Mary Miller was now a widow and the sole proprietor of the Goldstream Hotel. She was known affectionately as "Ma" Miller—a no-nonsense woman blessed with a strong measure of common sense. Ma Miller hired her niece, Daisy Cairns, to help her manage the hotel, and the two certainly had their hands full, particularly on the day when a special E&N excursion train brought three hundred children and their teachers from St. Mary's Sunday school in Oak Bay for an all-day party. Miller and Cairns worked tirelessly to provide the kids with a tasty lunch and a fun experience. The kids were disappointed when it came time to leave, but I'm sure that Miller and Cairns had a good rest after such an exhausting day.

Such was the nature of Ma Miller and her dedication to her career as a hotel operator and hostess, and it earned her the respect of her guests and the community. Her reputation continued to shine when she attempted to save the lives of a Mr. King and his daughter, who ran into trouble while swimming in the Goldstream River. When Miller learned what was going on, she immediately alerted a road crew working nearby, and they rushed to pull the unconscious pair out of the river and try to resuscitate them. Keeping a cool head, Miller contacted the provincial police and ambulance service, but unfortunately, the man and his daughter could not be revived. During the inquest into the tragic accident, Ma Miller received honourable mention for her part in trying to save the two victims.[66]

In January 1923, the Goldstream Hotel was destroyed by fire. Evidently wanting to remain in the hotel business, Miller purchased the Colwood Hotel, which she ran for six years (see page 26). In May 1929, she married A.C. Smith, a local horse breeder and former horse jockey. They kept and raised race horses on their farm in Goldstream.

In 1930, the couple sold the Colwood Hotel to George T. Quincy and spent the money building the new Goldstream Inn and beer parlour across the street from the original hotel site. A few outbuildings that had survived the 1923 fire were moved to form part of the new inn. After overcoming opposition to their application for a beer parlour licence, Mrs. Miller-Smith operated the inn and beer parlour successfully from 1930 to 1946. The beer parlour is reputed to have had an interesting system for customers to use when ordering beer: when a customer wanted a round of beer, they would press a buzzer that was on or near their table. I'm not sure how long that system lasted, but Ma Miller's Pub is alive and well to this day.

The third version of the Goldstream Inn, known as Ma Miller's because of the effervescent owner Mary "Ma" Miller, who built the hotel in 1930. Photograph by the author, 2015.

SHAWNIGAN LAKE
MILE 45

COWICHAN BAY
MILE 61

CHAPTER 2

Shawnigan Lake to Cowichan Bay

THE NORTHBOUND TRAIN WAITED PATIENTLY at Goldstream Station until the whistle blew, alerting passengers to the final boarding. As the last passenger scrambled aboard, the train slowly steamed out of the station to begin its long gradual ascent up the Malahat.

It was easy going through the Goldstream valley until the train came to the first of a series of creeks and ravines traversed by wooden trestles. The 550-foot trestle over Waugh Creek near Goldstream Park—in use from 1886 until 1908, when the track was realigned, and the bridge was demolished[1]—gave passengers an idea of what was to come. Other trestles quickly followed, including the 365-foot span over Goldstream Creek, the 110-foot curved trestle above two streams called Double Head Ravine, and the biggest challenge for the E&N construction team, the impressive trestle that crossed over Niagara Canyon at mile 14, where at the centre it was a terrifying 230 feet to the ground. The 190-foot Arbutus Canyon Bridge trestle was the last before the push to the summit.

The train engine laboured as it started up the seven-hundred-foot steep grade of Arbutus Bluff, leaving a trail of thick black smoke behind as it climbed. Then came the one and only tunnel on the route. The children pressed their noses against the windows to see the grand view of Saanich Inlet that was revealed at the tunnel's exit. In a series of sporadic jerks, the train finally reached the summit, 916 feet above sea level. In the summer, when the train carried up to three hundred tourists attending events at Shawnigan Lake, two locomotives were required to push it up and over the summit.

On the gradual downhill run to the lake, the train emerged from the shadows of the thinning Douglas firs and flashes of light began to spill into the passenger cars from the summer sun. Lucky travellers caught their first glimpse of Shawnigan Lake, shimmering from the reflection of the sun's rays on sky-blue water and filling both children and adults with awe and excitement. The train slowed as it rounded a corner and the Morton House came into view.

The whistle blew, announcing the arrival of the afternoon train at Shawnigan Lake. Curious travellers peered out from the coach windows at the Morton House, the new hotel by the lake. The train slowed to a stop before the passengers disembarked and stretched their legs after the one-and-a-half-hour journey from Victoria. In the summer of 1899, a regular round-trip ticket for the twenty-eight-mile journey from Victoria to Shawnigan Lake cost seventy-five cents for adults and forty-nine cents for children.[2]

MORTON HOUSE (KOENIG HOTEL, SHAWNIGAN LAKE HOTEL)
1886–1916

In 1886, the experienced and popular Victoria hotelier Charles Morton was watching the progress of the E&N Railway construction with interest when he saw the opportunity to purchase an existing house by Shawnigan Lake and renovate it into a resort hotel for holiday travellers. His Morton House opened on November 20, 1886, three months after Sir John A. Macdonald drove in the last spike at Cliffside, less than a mile from the hotel, signifying the

A Famous Tourist and Fishing Resort,
The Koenig Hotel,
Koenig, Shawnigan Lake, British Columbia.

Koenig's Hotel, Shawnigan Lake, E. & N. Ry.
Vancouver Island, B. C.

Shawnigan Lake Hotel, Vancouver Island, B. C.
Mrs. George Koenig, Proprietress.

completion of the E&N Railway, and less than a month after the first regular train travelled the seventy-two miles from Nanaimo (mile 0) to Victoria.[3] The E&N was responsible for opening up Shawnigan Lake and other previously inaccessible communities, and it was critical to the success of the Morton House.

Born in 1830 in Jersey, the largest of the Channel Islands, and educated in England, Charles Morton was thirty-two when he packed his bags and joined the thousands of hopeful prospectors attempting to make their fortune in the Cariboo gold rush. While he didn't exactly strike it rich, he did make enough money in the ten years he was in the Yale District to buy a hotel in Victoria. He owned the Angel Hotel on Langley Street from 1872 to 1873 and was elected as a municipal councillor in 1873. He was also well connected with the business community, once holding the office of Noble Grand of the Victoria Lodge of the Odd Fellows.[4]

The call of the Cariboo lured Morton to leave Victoria in March 1880. He leased a hotel at Spences Bridge before building his first Morton House, which opened on July 1, 1881. (The Morton House at Shawnigan was his second.) In March 1883, Morton sold his hotel to the partnership of Bligh and Tait and returned to Victoria.[5]

Morton was willing to try different things, and his next venture was opening a stationery store on Government Street in downtown Victoria in 1884, where he imported books, newspapers, periodicals, cutlery, and fancy stationery.[6] In July he was elected as a new member of the Board of Trade of British Columbia, but within a year, Morton was forced to sell his stationery store due in part to ill health caused by a weak heart.[7] Despite this, he decided to return to the hotel business by either purchasing a hotel or building a new establishment somewhere along the E&N line, and this ultimately brought him to Shawnigan Lake.

Facing page, top to bottom: The Morton House became the Koenig Hotel in 1891 and continued to prosper on the shore of Shawnigan Lake. Postcard from the author's collection; Another hand-tinted colour postcard of the Koenig Hotel taken around 1902. Note the railroad tracks right out front of the hotel. Postcard from the author's collection; The Koenig Hotel became the Shawnigan Lake Hotel. Postcard from the author's collection.

A month after the gala opening of his second Morton House that promised customers "charming scenery, a beautiful lake, and fine climate," Morton expanded with a fifty-by-thirty-foot addition.[8] On Good Friday, April 8, 1887, a series of special excursion trains were added to the regular E&N schedule as Morton organized a "Grand Angling Competition" in which the winner received a prize of twenty-five dollars presented by Charles Morton and the Morton House. A rifle-shooting competition was also held on these occasions. Guests to the hotel could hire a boat for the day or the hour, and a large one-hundred-by-eighty-foot covered dance floor was built outdoors for the evening's entertainment.[9]

The summer of 1887 proved to be special, as it was the first summer that travellers could access beautiful Shawnigan Lake so easily (and at a low cost) thanks to the E&N. Recreational activities included swimming, fishing, boating, picnicking, and simply relaxing by the cool blue waters. Businesses and other organizations, such as the Odd Fellows of Victoria, organized return excursion trips featuring a picnic and regatta on Shawnigan Lake followed by a dance and dinner at the Morton House, all for the rate of $1.25 for adults and twenty-five cents for kids under ten.[10] These seasonal outings to the lake were well attended and quickly became annual events.

Morton's hunch to open a hotel at Shawnigan paid off handsomely. His genuine hospitality and attention to detail in such a beautiful natural setting gave him all the business he could handle. But as he started planning for the 1891 season, he began feeling tired and ill. Concerned that perhaps all of his hard work preparing for and looking after his guests was putting a strain on his heart, Morton bought a ticket on the noon train to Victoria on January 3, 1891, to see his doctor at St. Joseph's Hospital. He died en route, reportedly somewhere near Goldstream. Dr. Morrison performed a post-mortem exam of the body and determined that the sixty-year-old Morton had died from "a clot of blood upon the heart."[11] The funeral was held the following day at Christ Church Cathedral, and Morton was laid to rest at Ross Bay Cemetery.

The Morton House, including all furnishings, boats, and boathouse, was put up for sale by Morton's agent on Wharf Street, and Henry Short became the temporary manager of the hotel until new owners were found. In the summer of 1891, George and Mary Ann Koenig purchased the popular Morton House and renamed it the Koenig Hotel—though a few of the old-timers at the bar still referred to it by its original name, or simply as "Morton's."

The Koenigs proved to be a good fit as they continued the tradition of fine service begun by Charles Morton. Said one respected athlete who was participating in an oarsman competition on Shawnigan Lake while staying at the Koenig Hotel, "If the treatment I receive here continues then I will not want to leave the lake."[12] But just when things were going well for the German hosts and their first summer season operating the hotel was exceeding their expectations, Mary Ann Koenig died from complications during childbirth. Like Morton's, her funeral took place at Christ Church Cathedral in Victoria and she was buried at Ross Bay Cemetery.[13]

George Koenig met and married his second wife, Anna, in the autumn of 1892, and in the last decade of the nineteenth century, the Koenig Hotel thrived. Each summer season saw the hotel filled to capacity, or close to it. The revenue generated from the business allowed the Koenigs to enlarge the hotel in 1897, and on its schedules, the E&N even changed the name of the first northbound stop at Shawnigan Lake to "Koenig's." On July 23, 1899, the annual summer picnic normally held at Goldstream was moved to Shawnigan Lake. Some three hundred people attended, many staying overnight at the Koenig Hotel.[14] The place was as popular as ever during these happy years, but like the saying goes, all good things come to an end.

The end for the Koenig Hotel arrived on the afternoon of December 16, 1901. According to news reports, the family was sitting down for lunch when a crackling noise was heard in an adjoining room. When George Koenig opened the door to investigate, he was met by a wall of smoke and flames. Seeing that it was too late to attempt to extinguish the flames, he ordered the family to begin removing as much furniture as they could save. Fortunately, the E&N freight train had just arrived, and when the crew saw the smoke billowing out of the hotel, they jumped from the train and began helping the Koenigs to salvage as much as possible before the flames completely consumed the hotel.[15]

George and Anna decided to rebuild, replacing the old charred ruins of their Koenig Hotel with the larger and more elegant Shawnigan Lake Hotel. Opening informally on May 25, 1902, the new hotel boasted cottages, a store, a post office, and a small attached train station. The formal reopening on Saturday, June 7, 1902, featured a basketball game and a ping-pong tournament, followed by an elaborate dinner and dance in the spacious and spectacular new ballroom.[16]

The morning after the gala-opening celebrations, George went for his morning bath in the Shawnigan Lake, as was his habit. Having never learned to swim, he normally kept quite close to shore. When he didn't return, his wife went to fetch him, only to discover his lifeless body lying in the shallow water. The subsequent inquiry into his death concluded that there was no foul play, nor was there evidence of suicide; rather, it was officially deemed that George Koenig had died by accidental drowning.[17]

With Anna Koenig now the sole owner of the Shawnigan Lake Hotel, the dances in the lovely ballroom continued, as did the E&N excursion train service to the very popular events held at Shawnigan Lake each summer, such as the regatta, the company and labour picnics, and the sports fishing derby.

In December 1912, Anna Koenig sold the hotel for $50,000 to James Finlay, who hired D.J. McSweyn, late of the Fink Mercantile Company Clothing Store in Cranbrook, as manager.[18] With help from her sons George and Harry, Anna continued to operate the general store that had once been a part of the hotel. In May 1915, after the sinking of the RMS *Lusitania* by a German submarine during the First World War, Anna and her sons changed their

German surname from Koenig to Kingsley.[19] Mrs. Kingsley died in 1948, but by this time, her former hotel was long gone. In the early morning hours of August 22, 1916, the Shawnigan Lake Hotel was destroyed by fire.

A room with a view of Shawnigan Lake from the Strathcona Hotel. Postcard from the author's collection.

STRATHCONA HOTEL
1900–1927

While the Koenig Hotel was enjoying its monopoly in the resort business at Shawnigan Lake, a group of investors was planning a rival venture. The Shawnigan Lake Hotel Company was formed in 1900 by a group of prominent Victoria businessmen who managed to obtain from the E&N Railway a ninety-nine-year lease on a site overlooking Strathcona Bay. They commissioned renowned

Strathcona Hotel at Shawnigan Lake in 1916 when the CPR purchased the hotel and added a railway station. Image 2010-010-139 courtesy of the Oak Bay Archives.

architect Samuel Maclure to design their new Strathcona Hotel in consultation with his business partner, C.J. Soule;[20] Fred Sherbourne was hired to build the hotel for approximately $14,000.[21]

As it neared completion, the resort hotel took on a look and feel of permanence and was the epitome in luxury resorts. The thirty-one-room, three-storey Strathcona Hotel was built on fifty acres of landscaped lakeside lawns, with both tennis courts and a boat launch in the plans. The carpenters were adding the final fancy finishing touches prior to the May 15, 1900, grand opening when disaster struck.

Before vacationers could have a chance to enjoy the magnificent structure, it was totally destroyed by a fierce fire.[22] Undaunted by this sudden setback, the Shawnigan Lake Hotel Company partners agreed to rebuild. From the ashes came the second Strathcona Hotel, just as ornate and elaborate as the first, but with special care taken to ensure that this hotel would not meet the fate of its predecessor.

Built on the side of a hill overlooking Shawnigan Lake, the Strathcona finally opened on September 19, 1900. The E&N Railway was located immediately behind the hotel, which proved convenient for guests and day trippers. "As visitors alighted from the train they entered an impressive portico which led to the lobby of the hotel. The elegant and luxurious hotel boasted thirty-one bedrooms, two dining rooms, two drawing rooms, a sitting room and a smoking room. The grounds were beautifully landscaped and a promenade bridge was built across Strathcona Bay to the peninsula on the other side. A boat house with a dance pavilion was situated on the lakeshore."[23]

Just imagine what it must have felt like to stroll along the wide wraparound veranda of that great Victorian hotel, gazing out at acres of immaculately groomed verdant lawns; watching other guests enjoying a leisurely game of croquet, or observing a foursome engaged in a tennis match; feeling the cool breeze off the lake, upon which were all types of watercraft—all the while hearing the muffled shrieks of joy rise up the hill from the children swimming and playing at the nearby beach. Imagine coming upon a cozy wicker chair that invited you to sit for a spell and relax as you let the sights and sounds of summer wash over you. Such was the lot of happy vacationers who experienced the rejuvenating power of this splendid resort.

Experienced hotelier William E. Green was the first manager of the Strathcona Hotel from 1900 to 1902. Green and business partner Thomas J. Martin had operated the popular Windsor Hotel in Nanaimo from 1896 to 1900, when they had a falling out. In November 1903, the Shawnigan Lake Hotel Company sold the Strathcona Hotel to Mrs. J.E. Wark, formerly of the first-class Burdett House in Victoria, where she had enjoyed a good reputation. With her husband by her side, Wark undertook some renovations to the hotel, changing the upstairs dining room into a drawing room, adding a new and larger dining room downstairs, and adding new bedrooms and bathrooms as well as a new bar to greet guests disembarking from the train platform at the rear of the hotel. The new owners also decided to keep the hotel open year-round as opposed to operating it as only a summer resort.[24]

Mrs. Wark organized evening concerts at the hotel during the summer season. For the special price of only fifty cents, one could purchase a round-trip ticket from Victoria to the Strathcona Hotel aboard the E&N, enjoy a scrumptious dinner, and listen to music provided by the Fifth Regiment band.[25] It must have been marvellous to sit on a blanket on the grass in the warm evening listening to the band play in such a salubrious setting. Picnics were also popular at the lake throughout the summer season, and a variety of games and activities like baseball and tug-of-war kept families entertained.

By 1911, the Malahat Highway had been substantially improved, allowing safer access to Shawnigan Lake by automobile. At first the E&N Railway was not threatened by the completion of the highway; most people couldn't afford an automobile, and train travel was more affordable for the average family. It wasn't until regular bus service was introduced in the 1930s that the railroad faced any serious competition.

The Warks successfully ran the Strathcona Hotel until 1912, when they sold it on the eve of the First World War, and Herbert Cancellor became the new manager. Cancellor was the proprietor of the Cameron Lake Chalet just off the Alberni Road before coming to the Strathcona.

In 1916, the Canadian Pacific Railway (CPR) purchased the Strathcona for the purposes of making it a railway station hotel to replace the one lost to fire at the Shawnigan Lake Hotel earlier that year.[26] (The CPR had purchased the E&N Railway from Robert Dunsmuir's son, James Dunsmuir, in 1905, and already owned the land that had been leased to the original owners of the Strathcona.) Hebert Cancellor, meanwhile, went into a partnership with his relatives, Mr. and Mrs. Fred Cancellor of the Glenshiel Inn in Victoria, and purchased the Brentwood Hotel on Saanich Inlet.[27]

By 1920, the hotel was known as the Strathcona Lodge and was leased from the CPR by M.A. Wylde. It boasted forty rooms, all with hot and cold running water and private baths (American plan), as well as three hard-surface tennis courts, boat rentals, a putting green, and croquet—all for $3.50 per day or $21 per week.

In September 1926, just as the summer season was wrapping up, Victoria Wylde, daughter of the proprietor, was enjoying the mild summer air from the veranda when she heard shouts from the lake for help. Four men, all employees of the Shawnigan Lake Lumber Company, had rented a boat from the Strathcona Lodge and were rowing to the logging camp on the other side when their boat overturned and threw the men into the water. None were wearing flotation jackets at the time. Victoria immediately alerted her father, who wasted little time in setting out on the lake with his own boat to search for the men. It was past ten-thirty in the evening and growing quite dark when he finally spotted the boat about halfway across the lake. As Wylde approached the overturned craft, he could see two men clinging to it—one at the bow and one at the stern. Both men were exhausted and in shock from the ordeal, and as Wylde was rescuing the man clinging to the bow, the other man could no longer hang on and disappeared under the surface of the lake, becoming the third drowning victim that night. If it wasn't for the quick actions of Mr. Wylde and his daughter, there would have been four fatalities.[28]

In May 1927, it was announced that the Strathcona Lodge would no longer operate as a hotel. Under the direction of new owner Miss Minna Gildea, it was converted into the Strathcona School for Girls, and it operated as such until 1969, when the stately building was demolished.

STATION HOTEL (WILTON PLACE)
1891–1942

It was a delightful ten-minute train ride from the Strathcona Hotel with its train station attached at Shawnigan Lake to the south Cowichan Valley and the unincorporated village of Cobble Hill.

Across from the modest Cobble Hill Station sat the appropriately named Station Hotel, so travellers didn't have far to go for a comfortable room, a hot meal, and a good stiff drink.

Europeans first settled in the Cobble Hill area around 1850, initially arriving along ancient footpaths made by Indigenous peoples, and then by horse and buggy along primitive roads. The area was heavily forested with a scattering of farming homesteads, and settlers at Cobble Hill relied on the rough road to Harrisville (Cowichan Bay) for their supplies, which arrived by ship and were transferred to Cobble Hill by wagon. The community developed very slowly until the arrival of the E&N Railway in 1886, and with it a reliable transportation link to Victoria and Nanaimo that helped grow the community. "Today's road network reflects the historic layout of the community in which all trails and roads in the area led to the railway station. It was a main focal point of the community; even the first post office operated out of an old boxcar."[29]

In 1891, the Porters were running the general store and post office in Cobble Hill when James Porter built the Station Hotel across the tracks from the train station. The two-storey wood structure had an impressive entry hall that featured an ornate grand piano and was often used for singalongs, recitals, and special occasions. There were rooms for both the drinker and the teetotaller at opposite ends of the hotel, and several rooms on the second floor offered splendid views of the village and the countryside. Known colloquially as the Cobble Hill Hotel, the Station Hotel was a pleasant country inn set on a large tract of land reported to be between "43 to 100 acres, more or less."[30]

On January 22, 1893, the Porters gave their daughter, Alice, a wonderful wedding reception at the hotel. Alice married "a thriving young farmer from the area," James Alexander, in a colourful ceremony followed by a "sumptuous breakfast in which 40 guests

Typical sporting scene,
Cobble Hill, Vancouver
Island, B. C.

T. N. Hibben & Co., Victoria B.C.

partook." In the afternoon, the happy couple boarded the train amid the traditional shower of rice and departed for their honeymoon in Victoria.[31]

The Porters ran the Station Hotel until the end of 1907, when they sold it to Mr. and Mrs. Nelson La Croix (variations of the surname included Le Croix and Lacroix). A few months later, in February 1908, the La Croix family went through a crisis when their infant son died while in care at St. Joseph's Hospital in Victoria. The little boy was laid to rest in the Cobble Hill churchyard.[32] La Croix put the business up for sale the following year, but there were no takers.

In April 1910, Nelson La Croix died, and the hotel (along with the rest of his estate, including the general store, house, outbuildings, and land) once again went up for sale. The partnership of Sidney Booth and Percival T. Stern purchased the Station Hotel and ran it successfully until Prohibition in October 1917 caused the significant revenue from the bar to dry up.[33] The hotel closed until August 1920, when partners Arthur H. Napper and Clifford D. Machlin reopened it.

The new owners renamed the Station Hotel Wilton Place and renovated it to add more rooms and enlarge existing ones. Adding to the charm of the country inn was a lattice fence running along the front attached to a lattice arbour leading to a flight of stairs and the main entrance of the hotel.

Alcohol prohibition in British Columbia lasted from October 1, 1917, until June 1921, when government liquor stores opened, but one could not enjoy a drink in a bar until March 1925, when the first beer parlour licences were issued. Meanwhile, in November 1922, Wilton Place was raided by the BC Provincial Police, which seized a quantity of illegal booze. The hotel's new proprietor, a man by the name of Herbert Macklin, was ordered to appear in provincial court in Duncan to plead to the charges.

It seemed like all was forgiven when the government Liquor Control Board granted the owners of Wilton Place, Herbert and

Ethel J. Macklin, one of the first beer parlour licences, in March 1925.[34] But it must have felt like one step forward and three steps back when Herbert Macklin was again in a Duncan court before Judge McIntosh, charged under the Indian Act for serving liquor to an Indigenous person.[35] He was ordered to pay a fifty-dollar fine. Aside from a few headaches caused by the strict liquor regulations, the hotel ran smoothly.

Herbert was born in the late 1870s in the small English town of Harnham just outside Salisbury, where his father was elected mayor during the First World War. After receiving his education in England, he immigrated to Alberta and stayed with relatives until 1896, when he moved to Victoria, British Columbia. That's where Macklin met the love of his life, Ethel Crockford, and within two years the couple married in a quiet ceremony at St. Mary's Church on Mayne Island. They built a lovely house on Rockland Avenue in Victoria, but they weren't in it long before they moved to Galiano Island. Herbert ran the post office there for a few years before they were on the move again, this time to Ladysmith, where he was hired as the manager of the local Simon Leiser Company Store. He quickly worked his way up to became general manager, and the family returned to Victoria, where the firm's head office was located. They stayed there until about 1922, when they moved, for the last time, to Cobble Hill. Shortly after their arrival, the Macklins purchased Wilton Place.[36]

Wilton Place was known for its excellent and inexpensive breakfast, lunch, high tea, and dinner. Special holiday packages were offered for groups, such as hunting parties, and the hotel's location across from the train station made it very convenient for travellers, as the bell hop was available to carry suitcases and bags from the station to the inn.

In January 1933, Herbert Macklin died after a brief illness at Cobble Hill, leaving Ethel as proprietor of Wilton Place, along with four daughters and a son.[37] The funeral service was held a few days later at Hayward's Funeral Parlour in Victoria, followed by interment at Ross Bay Cemetery.[38]

From 1934 to 1940, Wilton Place saw three owners come and go until H. Mighton bought the hotel in 1941. He was to be the last owner. On December 2, 1942, Wilton Place, a landmark at Cobble Hill for over fifty years, met the fate of many historic hotels when it was destroyed by fire. It was local storekeeper George Bonner's watchdog that sounded the first alarm.[39] When the dog smelled the smoke coming from a section of the nearby hotel, it began barking loudly and caught the attention of the storekeeper. Bonner immediately called the telephone operator, who notified the police and fire station. Despite the efforts of local residents and the Shawnigan Lake firefighters, the hotel burned to the ground. Underinsured and unable to overcome losses amounting to $20,000, the hotel was not rebuilt.[40]

BUENA VISTA HOTEL

1908–1956

The E&N train whistle beckoned passengers to board for the thirty-minute journey from Cobble Hill to Cowichan Station, a lumber,

Cowichan Station, Vancouver Island, British Columbia.

fishing, and farming community set in the lovely, green Cowichan Valley. After passing through rolling farmlands interspersed with groves of Douglas fir, the train slowed into the station, where passengers booked to stay at the Buena Vista Hotel at Cowichan Bay were met by the hotel stagecoach.

Cowichan Bay's history of European settlement began in 1859, when Samuel Harris arrived and built two cabins on the seashore. One of the cabins became the John Bull Inn. More settlers began arriving in the early 1860s, and slowly a community grew up around the inn, including a wharf, a general store, a post office, a church, log houses, and a makeshift jail.[41] Connected to Victoria via regular steamship service, the Cowichan Bay area was very popular with hunters and sports fishermen, and over time, a number of hotels and resorts also opened to cater to the seasonal influx of tourists—including the Buena Vista Hotel.

The Bay Hotel originally opened in 1905 as a short-lived addition to G.B. Ordano's general store and reopened as the Buena Vista Hotel in April 1908, just in time for the summer season. Guests staying at the new hotel during its first weekend of operation, including I. Tait, R.R. Smith, and R.L. Pocock of Victoria, were rather pleased with their stay when they left for home with a number of baskets filled with trout and salmon.[42] The Buena Vista launched a regular advertising campaign that simply read, "How's the fishing? GOOD," but it was mostly word of mouth that caused sports fishermen to flock to the hotel to bring home their own baskets full of fish. The hotel also invited hunters to stay, providing them with maps of the best hunting spots in the region.[43]

With the E&N Railway in close proximity, Buena Vista manager N. Brownjohn provided a daily stagecoach (later replaced by an autobus) to greet guests arriving by train at Cowichan Station. From there it was an easy two-and-a-half-mile journey to the

Facing page: Hand-tinted colour postcard of Cowichan Station, a stop along the E&N between Cobble Hill and Cowichan Bay. Postcard from the author's collection.

charming two-storey Buena Vista Hotel, a relatively large wood building that offered guests a spacious dining room, a well-stocked bar, and large, comfortable rooms, each with a splendid view of Cowichan Bay.[44] A wraparound balcony off the main floor allowed guests to take in some air or sit back and watch the boats on Cowichan Bay.

In addition to renting rooms and providing boats and gas for those who wished to take advantage of the excellent salmon fishing, the hotel rented out waterfront campsites. These sites became very popular with the vacationing public and were filled to capacity each summer season.

From 1910 to 1920, hotel management changed four times, but the Cowichan Bay Hotel Company Ltd., operated by Beatrice and Athelstan (Athel) Day, retained ownership until 1930. While fishing drew the greatest number of guests, other activities included the annual Dominion Day regatta held in Cowichan Bay, followed by a grand fête, dinner, and dancing at the Buena Vista Hotel, in conjunction with activities held at the Cowichan Station hall.[45]

Retired Major L.G. Fanning owned the hotel from 1930 to 1934 during the dark days of the Great Depression, when almost everyone coped with less. The Buena Vista was not immune to the effects of the economic downturn. Prior to the start of the 1933 season, Major Fanning found himself before a judge to plead for a delay in an order of foreclosure on the mortgage held against the hotel. The order was temporarily stayed, giving Fanning time to get his financial house in order to open for the season.[46]

In 1935, F. Saunders became the proprietor of the Buena Vista, and he remained the proprietor for the next five years as effects of the depression lingered on. It took the outbreak of the Second World War in September 1939 to get the economy back on its feet, but the Buena Vista Hotel's challenging days were not yet over.

On November 21, 1939, just a few months after Canada followed Britain into the war, a fire broke out in the annex of the seventeen-room Buena Vista Hotel. A passenger about to board the Cowichan Bay bus first spotted the smoke and sounded the alarm, but despite catching the fire in its early stages, the local fire department and neighbours were unable to prevent the blaze from devouring the annex building. Fortunately, the forestry department contributed a seawater pump that stopped the flames from spreading to the main hotel building, and nobody was killed or injured in the fire, for the rooms in the annex had been closed for the off season. Still, this event was yet another example of how vulnerable wood structures, and especially old hotels, were (and still are) to the threat of fire.[47]

Once the fire was extinguished, an investigation into its cause suggested that it had started in the passageway leading from the main hotel to the annex. There was talk that the fire had been set on purpose, but there was no evidence to support that theory. After the charred timbers cooled, the remains of the annex were cleared away, and that portion of the hotel grounds sat empty for six years until Ray Castle, the new proprietor of the Buena Vista Hotel, built a new building.[48]

It's only appropriate that Castle was also president of the Cowichan Bay Coho Club, as sports fishing continued to be a big draw to both the hotel and Cowichan Bay. The Buena Vista Hotel became the headquarters for the rival Cowichan Bay Salmon Club, hosting their meetings, dinners, and occasional dances in its recently expanded and modernized facilities. The bar, called the Anglers Room, acted as the unofficial clubhouse for sports fishermen in the area, and as the night wore on, the fish tales would become more exaggerated. The hotel also had an international reputation for hospitality tied in with fishing, attracting Hollywood celebrities like Bob Hope, Bing Crosby, and John Wayne as guests.

The end came for the old hotel in October 1956, when it was consumed by the flames of a furious fire. Arson was suspected as the cause, as the owner at the time was seen removing the cash register from the hotel shortly before it went up in flames.[49] After the fire, the site sat empty until the Cowichan Bay Arms apartment building was erected, giving another generation a chance to enjoy the view.

DUNCAN
MILE 64

MOUNT SICKER
MILE 78

CHAPTER 3

Duncan to Mount Sicker

THE NORTHBOUND E&N TRAIN TOOK about fifteen minutes to travel from Cowichan Station to the lush green farming community of Duncan. Known today as the City of Totems, "Duncan rose from a small valley clearing on the long pack trail from Victoria being at first merely a break in the journey of early exploration . . ."[1]

The city took its name from William Chalmers Duncan (1836–1919), who arrived in Victoria from Sarnia, Ontario, in May 1862. In August that year, Duncan and seventy-eight other settlers arrived at Cowichan Bay aboard the Royal Navy vessel *Hecate*.[2] The independent Duncan set off alone to explore his new home, and after a long walk through a valley, he climbed a red cedar tree to get his bearings. He soon discovered that the land contained rich soil suitable for growing a variety of crops. He built his home and began farming on a piece of land he called Alderlea farm; the name was also used for the small but growing community nearby. Duncan married in 1876, and his son Kenneth became the first mayor of Duncan.

In August 1886, when the inaugural E&N train bearing Sir John A. Macdonald and Robert Dunsmuir came through the area, no stop was scheduled at Alderlea. However, a crowd of two thousand assembled around a decorated arch at Duncan's Crossing, the level crossing nearest Alderlea, and the train came to an unplanned stop.

The arrival of the E&N transformed Duncan from a tiny settlement to a growing city by bringing in people, freight, farm equipment, and other goods, and shipping out the harvest. The E&N also contributed to the growth of logging companies by providing a faster and cheaper way of transporting their logs and lumber to market. "Ports attracted business and business attracted settlement, [and] that's how Nanaimo, Ladysmith, Port Alberni, Campbell River had their beginnings, but Duncan, like many other settlements, grew and prospered by the arrival of the E&N Railway."[3] In *Henderson's BC Gazetteer and Directory for 1900–1901,* "Duncan's," as it was sometimes called, was described as "a station on the E&N Railway in the Cowichan District, forty miles north of Victoria . . . splendid fishing in the Cowichan river, very close to the station."[4] Thanks to the E&N Railway and the stubborn efforts of pioneers who insisted that there must be a train station in their community, the town of Duncan's Station was incorporated in 1912 (the name was officially changed to Duncan on July 1, 1926).

Along with goods and more settlers who built retail shops, schools, churches, and homes in the community, the E&N train brought tourists to Duncan and points north. To house the visitors, three significant hotels were built in Duncan between the years 1887 and 1901: the Alderlea, a rather raucous establishment for working men looking for a drink; the Quamichan, considered a good choice for commercial travellers selling their wares; and the Tzouhalem, the most luxurious of the three in its early days (perhaps surprising to those who remember the "Zoo" in its final years).

ALDERLEA HOTEL

1887—1942

Built in 1887, the Alderlea was the first of the three major historic hotels built in Duncan. The two-storey wooden building was situated on the brow of Duncan's Hill (the *low* brow, you might say, considering the character of the clientele), attached to an existing store operated by William Beaumont. Taking the same name as the farm owned by William Duncan, the Alderlea Hotel, and especially its bar, became known as the place where working men such as loggers, sawmill workers, tradesmen, and labourers drank their way to inebriation. They made the hotel their home away from home and the hotel bar their playground, "Duncan's equivalent to the raucous Mount Sicker Hotel [see page 74] or Lake Cowichan's fist-worn Riverside Hotel: smoky, collegial, fight-ridden, noisy, overpriced, ugly, skunky, in short a classic frontier-style bar."[5]

It was in that atmosphere that the no-nonsense Charles H. Dickie leased the Alderlea Hotel in September 1891. He knew how to handle pugnacious customers, and he took great delight in cleaning up the place. Dickie had a reputation of his own; he had worked for the E&N Railway until he was fired for threatening to stuff an engineer into the firebox. He subsequently made a fortune from copper mined at Mount Sicker, and this financed his lease of the Alderlea.

"Not Duncan's finest, [the Alderlea] had been run from the wrong side of the bar by its previous owner and required firm hands-on management,"[6] and Dickie was just the man for the job. "When necessary and their customers weren't looking, Dickie and his pugilistic partner, Lee, took turns watering the drinks."[7] Other shenanigans by Dickie and his encouragers included taking the sixty-pound cannonball used as a doorstop and placing it gently into the case of a distracted guest as they were checking out of the hotel, then sitting back and enjoying the resulting hilarity as the poor person attempted to lift it. On another occasion, someone distracted a departing guest while another nailed his bag to the floor. And a customer once left for Victoria with a sheepskin in place of a tailored suit in his suitcase.[8] In these pranks, Dickie was encouraged by his regular customers—practical jokers all. When the bartender complained that someone was stealing cigars kept in a jar near the bar, Dickie soon spied the culprit and set a trap for him. Dickie removed the tobacco from the core of a few of the stogies, replaced it with gunpowder, and put the cigars back into the jar. It was just a matter of time before the suspect stole a few of the modified cigars from the jar when the bartender's back was turned, then retired to a window seat to enjoy a drink and a smoke. When he lit up, the cigar blew up in his face and his head hit the window so forcefully that the window pane shattered.[9]

By January 1893, Dickie decided he needed a change from bashing the heads of burley, drunken loggers, so he put his lease of the hotel up for sale. D.H. Adams, late of the Royal Hotel in Nanaimo (see page 106), took over the lease the following month,[10] and Dickie leased the nearby and more reputable Quamichan Hotel until 1899. (He subsequently entered politics and was elected as a Member of the Legislative Assembly, and then as a Member of Parliament for the Nanaimo District in 1922. He remained involved in politics until he was defeated by a CCF candidate in 1935.)

Adams had leased the Alderlea Hotel for less than a month when it was nearly destroyed by fire. On the afternoon of March 4, 1893, the roof of the hotel caught fire and thick black smoke could be seen for miles. The fire was eventually put under control and then extinguished after numerous willing hands formed a line and passed bucket after bucket of water to fight the blaze.[11] The rafters and most of the roof had to be replaced at the cost of $250, but the hotel was saved.

Adams sold his lease to William Crutchiey in November 1893, and a host of other proprietors followed, including Thomas Pitt, co-founder of the Duncan Merchants and future mayor, from September 1899 to 1902; Joseph A. Rogers from March 1902 to 1904;[12] and Ted Stock, who took over in 1904 and enlarged the Alderlea to a total of sixteen spacious rooms, each with a bath, a toilet, and hot and cold running water.[13]

By April 1913, Alex Smith was running the Alderlea Hotel. When the two-storey Duncan Garage was erected between the Alderlea and Quamichan hotels that year, "the Alderlea faced south over Trunk road but that was changed when they built the Duncan Garage. They had to modify the front entrance to the hotel and also removed an addition to the right on Trunk rd."[14] In January 1914, the hotel's newest proprietor, Edward (Ted) Stock, hired Victoria architects Crawford Coates and Arthur Fleet to design a three-storey, sixteen-room brick addition, with a spacious storefront on the ground floor.[15]

Prohibition closed the lucrative Alderlea bar in October 1917, cutting off one of the main sources of revenue for the owners. The hotel never quite recovered, and by 1942 it was converted into a tearoom run by Mrs. J.O. Nicholls, with rooms for rent on the second floor. The Johnsons owned the Alderlea Hotel in the 1940s and 1950s, and in March 1969, the old hotel was demolished to make way for an automated car wash when the Duncan Garage was expanded.

QUAMICHAN HOTEL
1887—1927

A short half-block walk (staggering distance) from the Alderlea Hotel in Duncan, the Quamichan Hotel opened in 1887, taking advantage of the new E&N Railway located in front of its doors. Built and owned by Frank H. Price and his business partner, Percy F. Jaynes,[16] the Quamichan Hotel took its name from the traditional

Above, top to bottom: The Quamichan Hotel in 1888 with the Duncan railroad station outside the front door. Image 1989.10.2.10 courtesy of the Cowichan Valley Museum; the Quamichan Hotel ca. 1936. Image from the author's collection.

language spoken by the Coast Salish peoples—*kw'amutsun* or *qu'wutsun*, meaning "warm place."[17] Jaynes later sold his interest in the Quamichan to Ernest Price, Frank's brother.[18]

In 1891, the Price brothers sold the Quamichan Hotel to Joseph Daly, who in turn leased it out. That same year, a worker building an addition for the Quamichan Hotel slipped off the roof and landed hard on the ground. Fortunately, he sustained only minor injuries.[19] The Cowichan Valley had received a considerable amount of rainfall that winter, and this probably contributed to the soggy conditions on the roof. Flooding was a serious problem in Duncan during those early years, and the winter of 1915 would prove to be particularly severe.

From 1893 to 1899, our old friend from the Alderlea Hotel, Charles H. Dickie, leased the Quamichan Hotel. While Dickie seems to have left his antics and abuse of patrons back at the Alderlea, one minor incident at the Quamichan Hotel under Dickie's watch is worth noting. In December 1893, Constable James Maitland-Dougall was summoned to the court in Duncan to examine some goods in the possession of a Mr. Charles Robinson, who was accused of stealing clothing from guests staying at the Quamichan Hotel. The accused wisely decided to plead guilty when it came to the court's attention that he was actually wearing some of the stolen property at the time of his court hearing.[20]

H. Grieves bought the lease from Dickie in 1899, and the latter entered the political career described earlier. By this time, the Quamichan Hotel boasted two capacious and airy dining rooms that allowed seating for up to seventy-five guests; the first-class bar and popular billiards room were also large and roomy.[21] In 1901, Grieves went to California to convalesce from an illness. When he returned to Duncan, he learned that the Quamichan Hotel had burned down. Grieves simply didn't have the energy to rebuild, so

Facing page, top to bottom: Crowds seeing off the Canadian Scottish Regiment departing Duncan train station in 1943. Image 1992.2.3.1 courtesy of the Cowichan Valley Museum; along with a name change from the Quamichan to the Commercial, new owners felt that a design change was required in order to update the hotel. You can judge for yourself if that was a good idea. Postcard from the author's collection.

he decided to move to Victoria to manage the Imperial Hotel. His successors at the Quamichan were Fred H. and Mrs. A. Nelson, who leased the hotel from owner Joseph Daly.

Duncan was witnessing a building boom at the time; daily cartloads full of lumber moved along the roads to the many buildings under construction, including the new Quamichan Hotel rapidly rising upon the ashes of its predecessor.[22] The new two-storey Quamichan was designed by the prolific architect Thomas Hooper,[23] and Walter Ford, the contractor, added an artistic touch to both the interior and exterior of the remarkable hotel.

The new Quamichan Hotel opened in June 1902, with Harry Watson as manager of the hotel and Fred Nelson running the bar.[24] Nelson was still putting on the final touches in the bar when the hotel opened, and once the actual bar was installed—a beautiful solid oak piece complete with back mirrors—he gathered his friends and staff to celebrate the occasion with a large quantity of wine.[25]

The modern new hotel must have been an impressive sight, especially to the passengers of the E&N train that stopped practically at its doorstep. Rivalling—even perhaps surpassing—the Tzouhalem Hotel located across the tracks, the Quamichan was heated by forced hot air, and each of the twenty-one guest rooms came with a bath and full toilet facilities, as well as an electric bell for ordering room service. The hotel also included spacious sample rooms for commercial men to sell their wares, as well as new stables.[26]

The Quamichan Hotel saw four proprietors come and go between 1903 and 1920, each leaving their mark on the hotel: C.J. Tulk (1903–1904); F. Conruyt (1905–1910); Edward Stock (1911–1913); and Louisa Tombs (1913–1920). In March 1920, advertisements called for tenders to move the Quamichan Hotel; it turns out that the proprietor was looking to jack up the hotel in order to protect it from flooding and did not actually intend to move it to a different location.

George H. Hardy was the proprietor of the hotel from 1920 to 1926. Although Prohibition ended in 1921, it wasn't until March 1925 that the first beer parlour licences were granted. Hardy obtained a licence, but he still found himself before Stipendiary Magistrate James Maitland-Dougall on a liquor-selling charge in November 1925, and he was convicted and fined $300 plus costs, or three months in jail in default. He appealed the case to a higher court, but the results of that appeal are not clear.[27] Hardy left the Quamichan in 1926, and the following year, the name of the hostelry changed to the Commercial Hotel under Mr. E. Havens.

The Commercial Hotel continued on through the war years, into the 1950s, and through some very embarrassing renovations in the 1960s that totally changed the look of the hotel (see the post-card). In 1990, the nemesis of all wood structures—fire—destroyed the hotel. The land sat empty for a number of years until a third establishment, the Phoenix Hotel, was built on the site.

TZOUHALEM HOTEL
1901–1990

Named after Coast Salish Chief Tzouhalem, the Tzouhalem Hotel was owned and operated by brothers Frank and Ernest Price from 1901 to 1923. The brothers had also owned the Quamichan Hotel, and they had concluded there was room for a first-class establishment in the Cowichan Valley.

Opening on July 26, 1901, the Tzouhalem attracted mostly British gentlemen and their families. The hotel's location on the corner of Front Street (Canada Avenue) and Trunk Road in Duncan was also a stop along the E&N Railway, and most guests arrived by train for their stay. The Price brothers also owned the Lakeside Hotel at Lake Cowichan, and they organized a stagecoach to take guests from the doorstep of the Tzouhalem Hotel to the front entrance of the Lakeside for a few days of hunting and fishing, and then return them to the Tzouhalem to end their vacation.

"The three-storied, multi-gabled Tzouhalem was just steps away for train travellers . . . Typically Edwardian, its lobby and main

Tzouhalem Hotel, Duncan, V. I., B. C.

Photo by M. W. Thompson, Duncan, J. C.

staircase was an overdone mix of heavy furniture, doilies, hanging and potted plants, and stuffed animal heads."[28] It quickly became a popular tourist destination and earned a stellar reputation for its excellent cuisine and first-class service: "The Tzouhalem Hotel offered a breakfast of toast upon which was ladled kippers and grilled kidneys. The Tudor-style hotel became a favourite haunt of British gentlemen and their less numerous gentlewomen."[29] The photograph on page 71 shows Edith and Frank Price and their son Fred Price in 1908 on the stairs leading to the nineteen rooms on the second floor numbered one to twenty (there was no room number thirteen). Fred was born in the Tzouhalem Hotel in 1902. Many years later, Fred mentions the photograph and a few memories of the hotel he grew up in during an interview with Bill Evans.[30] An animal head, a heron, and a black bear skin can be seen in this photograph.

In 1911 the Price brothers doubled the size of the hotel with a twenty-two-room addition. The barroom was removed to the basement, and the original bar space was converted to a lounge

and sitting room. That same year, they hired Percy E. Odgers as manager. Odgers migrated from Australia to Duncan and managed the Tzouhalem for two years before his untimely death from a cerebral hemorrhage in 1913 at the age of fifty-one.[31]

The hotel survived the economic blow caused by Prohibition from October 1917 to June 1921. In 1923 the Price brothers leased the hotel to Thomas Berry. Three years later, the hotel was sold to Grant and Elizabeth Thorburn, who had previously operated hotels in Vancouver, Prince Rupert, and Vernon. Grant managed the hotel until his death in 1930, when his wife Elizabeth took over, with her son-in-law, Donald Butt, as manager, until 1953.

Through the 1960s and 1970s, the aging Tzouhalem was no longer the first-class hotel it once had been. The popular beer parlour, nicknamed "the Zoo," still made money for the owners, but it had a reputation as a rowdy and, at times, even dangerous place to imbibe. The daily hijinks in the Tzouhalem Hotel beer parlour, in addition to the goings-on in the one just across the tracks at the Commercial Hotel, gave Duncan a bad rap and the unflattering nickname of "Drunken Duncan"—not exactly the reputation that the town's upstanding citizens desired.

A fire in 1980 nearly destroyed the old landmark hotel, but quick action by local firefighters saved most of the structure, despite the fact that the interior sprinkler system had not been functioning for years. The hotel sustained $100,000 in damage, mostly on the top floor. The fire occurred shortly after a costly renovation ($70,000), and instead of financing yet another renovation, the owners decided to close the damaged upper section. They continued to run the 154-seat pub, and later that decade changed the name to the Duncan Inn in hopes of reviving the hotel's reputation, but everyone still called it the Zoo.

The end finally came in September 1990, when the once proud historic hotel was demolished over three days (see photograph in the Afterword). A parking lot now occupies the spot where the hotel once stood, but plans were afoot to build on the site in 2012. "Intercoast's Stephen Holland said Sunday that he wants to construct a historically-themed building, tentatively called 'The Alderlea,' featuring two commercial spaces and six live-work spaces on the ground floor plus twenty-four residential suites of a thousand square feet each upstairs."[32]

In May 1911 the E&N Railway, owned by the CPR since Dunsmuir sold it in 1905, built a railroad branch (subdivision) that stretched from Osborne Bay to Cowichan Lake. From Duncan the E&N continued north to Hayward Junction where the main line went north, and a subdivision went west to Hillcrest then to Mayo Siding (Paldi), Sahtlam, and ending at the community of Cowichan Lake and the Riverside Hotel. This was timber and farming country where communities like Mayo (the name changed in 1936 to Paldi), in which extensive logging operations and a sawmill owned and run by the amazing entrepreneur Mayo Singh, provided logs and lumber sent to the market by trains on the E&N.[33] On June 18, 1913, the first passenger train to rumble west along the Lake Cowichan subdivision left the E&N mainline at Hayward Junction.

MOUNT SICKER HOTEL
1901–1909

The northbound train journey from Duncan to the next major train stop in the Cowichan Valley at Westholme took about twenty minutes. After leaving Duncan Station, the train embarked on a short, pleasant journey through the green and undulating farmlands of the Cowichan Valley. At Haywood Junction, where the Cowichan Lake subdivision of the E&N was completed in 1912, passengers could travel west to Cowichan Lake, off the main line.

The northbound train trundled on until it made a brief stop in the farming community of Somenos to exchange mail bags and pick up and drop off passengers. Minutes later came a stop at Mount Sicker Siding, with Mount Sicker looming on the left.

For the passengers disembarking at Mount Sicker, the stagecoach ride started out well enough as the roads were generally

good and flat, but the real adventure began as the road narrowed through a series of twists and turns winding up to the mining town of Lenora. Dusty and dirty in the summer

months and muddy in the rainy season, the wild ride up the 2,300-foot Mount Sicker was not for the faint of heart, but once at the top, passengers were rewarded with a commanding view of the Cowichan Valley below.

The story of Mount Sicker, a booming mining town in North Cowichan, approximately nine miles north of Duncan, and the Mount Sicker Hotel began in the fall of 1895, when three American prospectors stumbled upon traces of gold, silver, and copper. They returned the following summer and staked four claims, which they named the Alice, Leona, Belle, and Gold Queen claims. The prospectors prepared to mine immediately, but just before they could put shovels into the ground, Mother Nature intervened.

That August, a devastating forest fire forced the stakeholders to run for their lives as their makeshift cabin, along with most of their equipment and goods, was consumed. Discouraged, the Americans abandoned their claims, and it looked as though the mining site at Mount Sicker would return to nature.

In the spring of 1897, local prospector Harry Smith was poking around the Mount Sicker area when he discovered, at the 1,400-foot level, a thirty-foot-wide outcropping of copper on the surface, which had been revealed by the earlier fire. Smith named the new strike Lenora, after his daughter.[34] As word got out about Smith's discovery, the ensuing rush resulted in sixty claims being filed at Mount Sicker. This was the start of the profitable, but short-lived, Mount Sicker copper boom.[35]

By 1900, there were three major mines at Mount Sicker: the Lenora, the Tyee, and the Richard III, and they all enjoyed an amazing return on their money. By March 23, 1901, the Lenora mine had shipped 11,867 tons of ore valued at $175,831.[36] Wagon roads were initially used to transport the ore down the mountain to smelters at Crofton and later at Ladysmith. Later, a new spur line connecting to the E&N Railway sped up the process considerably.

The three competing mines could have made an even larger profit and would have lasted a lot longer if they simply cooperated. But competition was fierce, and they chose not to coordinate their efforts. The competing factions even built separate towns on different sides of Mount Sicker, including several hotels. The Mount Sicker Hotel was owned by the British Columbia Development Company, which had started the Lenora mine, and the competing Brenton Hotel was owned by the Tyee Development Company, based in London, England.

In anticipation of the new Mount Sicker Hotel, the Victoria *Daily Colonist* reported, in April 1901, that it would "be a fine structure for a place like this and will be ready for business in about a month. The weather is beautiful and there is an air of contentment everywhere."[37] Opening in May, the ornate two-storey establishment was quite lavish inside and out, reflecting the optimism brought on by the mining boom and the hope that it would be around for many years to come. Henry Croft (from whom Crofton got its name) was hotel manager, and Wallace W. Berridge was the first proprietor. In June, Berridge applied for a liquor licence for the fancy bar located on the main floor of the hotel.

The Tyee Development Company's answer to the Mount Sicker Hotel was the Brenton Hotel. It wasn't as elaborate as the Mount Sicker, but the bar attracted just as many thirsty miners, especially on a Saturday night. The two hotels peacefully co-existed until one hot summer day in August 1905, when Joseph Bibeau, the Brenton's proprietor, became caught up in a tragic event that began at the Mount Sicker Hotel.[38]

Mining work was dangerous, and several fatalities had occurred in the five years since mining began at Mount Sicker. One of the victims was a miner named Campbell, and he left behind a wife and a young daughter when he died. Mrs. Campbell worked in the Mount Sicker laundry, where she was friends with a number of the miners and other townsfolk.

Thirty-five-year-old Fredrick (Fred) Charles Beech was one of hundreds of men hired to mine copper during the boom that lasted at Mount Sicker from 1900 until the ore gave out in 1907.[39] He had been a co-worker and friend of the late Mr. Campbell, and what started for Beech as sympathy for the widowed Mrs. Campbell soon grew into infatuation. As time went by, Beech did not hide his affection for Mrs. Campbell, but she didn't feel the same. As the still-grieving widow ignored and then discouraged Beech's advances, the love-crazed miner became frustrated. His frustration boiled into anger, and that anger exploded when Mrs. Campbell and another man, Mr. Hardy, appeared to be getting friendly. Filled with rage and bitterness, Beech decided to do something about the situation.

Retrieving his rifle and a large quantity of ammunition from his cabin, Beech made his way to the Mount Sicker Hotel, where

Mrs. Campbell and her daughter were boarding. It was a Sunday morning, and Beech knew that Mrs. Campbell liked to take tea on the porch of the hotel each Sunday. Mad with jealousy, he intended to shoot and kill both Hardy and Campbell that morning.

Crouching in a gully about two hundred yards from the hotel, his .38-55 lever-action Winchester rifle cradled in his arms, Beech watched as Mrs. Campbell, tea in hand, stepped out onto the porch. He took steady aim and pulled the trigger, but the bullet missed its mark and glanced off an oil lamp before ending up lodged in the wall of the hotel. A startled Campbell looked around, and upon seeing Beech with a rifle aimed directly at her, instinctively dropped to the floor just as another shot rang out, again narrowly missing her. At that moment, Campbell's daughter walked out onto the porch to see what the noise was all about and saw her mother lying on the floorboards of the porch. Recognizing Fred Beech in the gully, the little girl retreated back into the hotel screaming, "Mr. Beech is trying to kill my mother!" Several guests, including Mr. Hardy, jumped up and ran to the door to the outside porch, only to see Beech calmly reloading his rifle.

Three loud pops were heard all over the village, including at the bar of the nearby Brenton Hotel, whose proprietor, Joe Bibeau, came running out to see what was going on. Bibeau and Beech were friends, and the hotelman ran toward Beech, yelling at him to stop shooting and to lower his rifle. But in his jealous rage, Beech either didn't recognize Bibeau or was past caring, and he swung around and shot his friend in the abdomen. Wide-eyed Bibeau reeled around in an attempt to flee back to his hotel when a second shot rang out, striking Bibeau in the jugular and killing him instantly. His lifeless body dropped to the ground. Beech froze for a moment, evidently realizing what he had just done. He jumped up and disappeared into the bush.

Beech returned to his cabin and collected a few things, including more ammunition. He wrote a farewell note to the police, his co-workers, and his friends, then lastly to his lost love, Mrs.

Campbell. There were no regrets in his message. A few hours later, two constables showed up at Beech's cabin and found the note, but no sign of Beech.

The manhunt began.

The next day, the town was practically deserted when most of the citizens went to pay their respects to the well-liked Bibeau, whose funeral was taking place in Duncan. Meanwhile, with the aid of Indigenous trackers, three constables hunted for Bibeau's murderer. Constable Morton stood guard at the Mount Sicker Hotel in case Beech returned to the scene of the crime and attempted to harm Campbell and Hardy. Mrs. Campbell, too grief-stricken to attend the funeral, was in protective custody.

And sure enough, Beech did show up to take care of unfinished business. Still flush with anger and determined to exact his revenge, a desperate Beech approached the hotel just as Mrs. Campbell was nervously looking out one of the hotel windows. Beech spotted her and fired a shot.

The bullet parted Mrs. Campbell's hair, and she promptly fainted.[40]

Beech may have thought that he killed her, for he let loose a wild volley of rounds in the direction of the hotel, hitting the side boards and breaking the bar window. Hearing the gunshots, the constables searching for Beech emerged from a nearby copse of trees. Meanwhile, Constable Morton barricaded himself inside the hotel and prepared to return fire. Everyone else dove for cover.

As the policemen approached with guns drawn, Beech ignored their shouts to drop his rifle. Escape was impossible. Knowing he couldn't take on the constables and having no intention of being taken alive, Beech's last desperate act was to turn his rifle on himself and fire. When police later examined the stock of the dead man's rifle, they found a carved farewell message to his parents.[41]

The copper mines at Mount Sicker lasted for two more years after the tragic events of the summer of 1905. In September 1907, James Harvey, the hotel proprietor, transferred the business to John

Creedon, who became the last owner before the hotel closed. The following May, the hotel's furniture, fixtures, and anything else that could be carried out were sold at rock-bottom prices in a sheriff's sale.[42] By 1909, the yield of copper ore had dropped off significantly and there was very little activity at Mount Sicker, and by 1911, the remaining citizens had gone. The population once peaked at 1,800, but like most single-industry towns, its boom had rapidly been followed by its bust.

In 1911, Edwin J. Pinson bought what was left of the Mount Sicker Hotel for eight dollars. He also purchased a few of the houses for two dollars each.[43] Most of the buildings were stripped of their wood and their remains torn down, but the Mount Sicker Hotel stood, an empty shell, for many years after the town had been abandoned, slowly rotting away from neglect, the weather, and vandals, until it too returned to the ground on which it was built.

CHEMAINUS
MILE 82

LADYSMITH
MILE 93

Logging at Chemainus, Vancouver Island, B.C.

Chemainus was where raw logs would arrive by rail to be processed in the sawmill then loaded onto waiting ships for export. Postcards from the author's collection.

CHAPTER 4

Chemainus to Ladysmith

TRAVELLING ALONG THE E&N FROM Victoria to Nanaimo in the summer of 1890, Mrs. Little described in her diary the view out the window: "While proceeding to Nanaimo we passed through lovely scenery by train and I was especially delighted by the flourishing appearance of Chemainus."[1]

The community of Chemainus grew up around the lumber industry. The first sawmill, powered by an overshot waterwheel, opened in 1862.[2] In May 1879, Albion Iron Works of Victoria designed and built a larger sawmill to replace the original structure. The new mill building measured 40 by 137 feet and was capable of cutting timber up to 100 feet.[3]

In August 1885, Henry Croft (who later managed the Mount Sicker Hotel, and gave his name to the town of Crofton) and a partner named Henry Severne bought the sawmill for $23,000 to process the timber felled when clearing the Ladysmith townsite right down to the shores of Oyster Bay. Working a six-day workweek at eleven and a half hours per day, a common sawmill worker earned thirty-five dollars per month, while a skilled employee such as an edgerman in the mill made up to fifty dollars per month.[4]

In 1887, the name of the mill had changed to the Croft and Angus Sawmill to reflect its new owners. The mill was also upgraded in anticipation of the arrival of the E&N Railway, which would greatly boost production as the trains could carry raw logs from the bush to the mill considerably faster and in greater quantity. By November 1888, the E&N was unloading logs at Chemainus camp daily.

In September 1900, the Victoria Lumber and Manufacturing Company (VL&M) was continuing to harvest great stands of virgin timber up the hillside behind the new town of Ladysmith, and the logs were transported by rail to be processed in the mills at Chemainus.[5] According to an article in the *Daily Colonist* at the time, the VL&M mill on the shores of Horseshoe Bay was one of the most unique and complete on the continent. It was the most modern mill of its kind and employed a vast number of men in both the sawmill and in the logging camps. The output from the mill was 250,000 board feet per day. Mr. E.J. Palmer, manager of the mill, wanted to inform the public that there was plenty of work available to any man willing and able.[6] It was during these boom years that the Horseshoe Bay Hotel prospered and grew.

HORSESHOE BAY HOTEL
SINCE 1892

In 1892, Matthew (Matt) Howe was working at the Chemainus sawmill when he purchased a large parcel of land south of town, beside the E&N Railway, for the purposes of building his home and an adjacent hotel. Born in Norfolk, England, in 1846, Howe had immigrated to Canada in 1883 and come to Chemainus with a contract to install and operate the steam-powered machinery at the sawmill. A kindly chap, Howe had very little formal education and had taught himself the principles of electricity and mechanics—knowledge that would come in handy in his new hotel endeavour.

By April that year, a new road along the shoreline from the Chemainus sawmill allowed for easier access to Howe's property. Howe quit his job at the mill the day he opened the Horseshoe Bay Hotel, named after the original European name given to the community when Admiral Sir George Richards explored the area for the Royal Navy in 1858–59. To avoid confusion with Horseshoe Bay in West Vancouver, the town had eventually adopted the name of Chemainus.

Early customers at the hotel included sawmill workers, long-shoremen, sailors, loggers, farmers, and travellers who arrived on the E&N trains.[7] Initially operating the hotel by himself, Howe built a bell tower and attached a sign that read, RING FOR SERVICE. This allowed him to work on his property until he heard the call from the bell.[8] While sheep grazed on his large property, Howe and some hired workers built a pipeline from the hotel to Fuller Lake and installed a pump system to supply hotel guests with fresh water. The enterprising Howe also built a system for lighting his hotel and home with power generated by running water.

The two-storey hotel initially had six rooms, but expansion through the years brought that number to fourteen. The rates for room and board, at one dollar per day or six dollars for the week, were quite reasonable for the times. The hotel also had a first-class bar and billiards room. When granting Howe a liquor licence for the bar, the licensing board commented that there had been "no house of entertainment between Nanaimo and Maple Bay" until that time, and Howe had no problem renewing the licence. Fred Chatters, Howe's nephew and long-time bartender, remarked, "Rye was 75 cents a bottle, scotch $1.25, and the best French Brandy $1.50. Patrons were handed the bottle and helped themselves, but the average man was not greedy and took only an average sized drink."[9] There were no problems until October 1893, when Howe was charged with serving an Indigenous man. Howe was found guilty, but as this was his first offence, he was let off with a warning and an order to pay the court costs.[10]

The Horseshoe Bay Hotel gained an international reputation when, on November 10, 1900, John D. Rockefeller checked in. Ten days later, the renowned industrialist and philanthropist Andrew Carnegie was a guest when he toured the timberlands that he owned in the area. Perhaps they'd heard about the splendid fare served at the hotel? Mrs. E. Anketel-Jones recalled that the Horseshoe Bay Hotel was noted for its excellent wines, liquors, and cuisine: "Meals comprised of such succulent luxuries as venison, grouse, quail, pheasant, poultry, home-cured ham and bacon, which was supplied by the Inn's own farm, and cream so thick that a spoon could stand up in it."[11]

Howe proved a shrewd businessman, not only with the hotel, but also in other ventures. In 1905, when it looked as though the once productive copper mines at Mount Sicker were waning, Howe immediately sold his sixteen thousand shares at ten cents per share.[12]

Howe was a widower (his wife, Eliza, was the first to be buried in the Anglican cemetery), and in 1907, he married the tall and striking Emily Jane Collyer, who moved into the hotel with her son Arthur. Born in England, Emily had previously been married to a guardsman for Queen Victoria, and she herself had worked in the Queen's household at Windsor Castle.[13] The Collyer family had eventually immigrated to Savannah, Georgia, where Emily gave birth to two boys, Arthur and Charles.[14] When Mr. Collyer died, Emily and her sons had moved to Victoria, where they lived for three years before moving up island to Chemainus. To confuse matters, Emily continued to be referred to as Mrs. Collyer even after her marriage to Howe.

After the marriage, the hotel went through some decorative changes as Emily adorned the walls with signed pictures of Queen Victoria and photographs of British aristocracy. In addition to its stellar reputation for hospitality and for the excellence of its table, this royal flair gave the hotel some extra panache, and it must have been good for business. The marriage between Matt and Emily, however, must not have been so successful, because by 1909, Emily and her son Arthur were the owners of the Horseshoe Bay Hotel (with Arthur as proprietor), and Howe had moved out to Swallowfield Farm.[15]

Arthur Collyer and his wife, Cecily (née Gallant), ran the Horseshoe Bay Hotel for the next twenty years. Arthur took pride in his cellar filled with fine vintage wines, and the dinners at the hotel were much sought-after events. When Prohibition came along in October 1917, Collyer converted the hotel bar into an ice cream parlour, then turned it back into a beverage room when Prohibition was replaced with government control.

Arthur's mother, Emily, died in Seattle on September 7, 1923, while visiting her other son Charles and his family.[16] In October 1929, on the eve of the stock market crash that brought on the Great Depression, Collyer sold the Horseshoe Bay Hotel to Harrison Whitehead, and the Collyer family moved to Saanich. Born in England before immigrating to the United States, and then to Nanaimo to work in the coal mines, Whitehead had gained experience in the hotel industry when he ran the Six Mile House outside Victoria for a number of years. He owned and operated the Horseshoe Bay Hotel until 1937 and died in Nanaimo in April 1961 at the ripe old age of ninety-three.[17]

After Whitehead, a parade of owners came and went for the Horseshoe Bay Hotel through the years, including one-time mayor of Chemainus Gerry C. Smith who owned the hotel from 1945 to 1985, up to its current owner, Dave Prakash, who also owns the Green Lantern Inn in Chemainus, the Saltair Pub, and the Ladysmith Inn. The original building no longer stands (the current Horseshoe Bay Inn was built in 1939), but the hotel of the pioneer days is depicted in one of the many famous murals that showcase the history of Chemainus, the "Little Town That Did."[18]

LEWISVILLE HOTEL
SINCE 1891

Travelling less than two miles north from the Horseshoe Bay Hotel along the E&N we come upon the Lewisville Hotel, constructed in 1891 by Samuel (Sam) Girdlestone Lewis in the small community named after him, Lewisville, south of Chemainus.

Originally a teacher in Chemainus, Lewis had quit his position when the E&N came to town and gone to work for the railroad.

Lewisville Hotel, Chemainus, V.I.,
British Columbia.

Proprietor—S. J. HAGAN.

In 1889, he built a general store near the train station, then saved his money from the store profits to build the Lewisville Hotel. Lewis ran both the store and the

The Lewisville Hotel in 1910. The name was changed to the Green Lantern Hotel around 1930. Image from the author's collection.

hotel until it became too busy for him. Sam's son, Arthur Lewis, would later work for the owner of the Buena Vista Hotel in Cowichan Bay.

In 1901, Lewis leased the hotel to James Cathcart. He was a rarity, described as a quiet and reserved Irishman. Cathcart and his wife ran the hotel for six years, and in that time, they had four children, two daughters and two sons. After the Cathcarts left, the lease passed on to Samuel Hagen.

On March 10, 1907, a devastating fire broke out in the hotel at around ten in the evening. Thought to be from an explosion of a coal oil lamp, the blaze spread so quickly that Hagen and his guests were forced to jump for their lives through their second-floor room windows. Many, including Hagen, sustained injuries from the fall, but avoided being burned to death. Hampered by the lack of water pressure and the fact that the buildings were tinder-dry and burned so quickly, firefighters were unable to prevent the inferno from engulfing the hotel and spreading to the general store and nearby outbuildings, destroying everything in its path.

Though, incredibly, no one was killed, the total losses were estimated to be between $20,000 and $25,000, and the hotel was insured for only a fraction of that amount.[19] While Sam Hagen recovered from his injuries, his wife took over as proprietress to oversee the construction of the new Lewisville Hotel.

In March 1911, new proprietors named Roche and Weddell arrived from Duncan to run the Lewisville Hotel. Born at Newcastle-on-Tyne, England, Weddell was the nephew of William Smithe, seventh premier of British Columbia.[20] After coming to Canada in 1874, Weddell settled in the Cowichan District before coming to Chemainus to run the Lewisville Hotel with Roche. Their tenure lasted two years until William L. Howell became the proprietor in 1913. Weddell retired in Chemainus, where he lived for many years until his death in February 1935.[21]

By 1916, Mr. E. "Butch" Howe was operating the Lewisville Hotel. In an interview many years later, a regular customer, Tom Guilbride, recalled that the growing town was very lively in those days. The hotel bar never closed, and upstairs was a room—dubbed the "snake room"—reserved for customers who had had too much to drink and needed a place to sleep it off. Guilbride also remembered the day he returned after a four-year absence fighting in the Great War. "I walking [sic] into the Lewisville bar and Butch Howe looked up from behind the bar and said, 'You owe me a dollar and a half.' After four years! We both laughed and he poured me a drink."[22] Prohibition followed in October 1917, but the Lewisville Hotel managed to survive without the revenue from the bar.

On November 17, 1923, the newspapers reported that the Chemainus sawmill had been destroyed by fire. Plans to replace the mill were drawn up during the cleanup of the debris. In March 1925, both the Horseshoe Bay and the Lewisville hotels were granted beer parlour licences after making some modifications to comply with the liquor regulations of the day.

From 1928 to 1931, the Lewisville Hotel went through a number of changes, including a name change to the Green Lantern Hotel under new proprietor Frank Crucil.[23] Frank and his wife, Mary, had arrived in town from nearby Ladysmith in 1924, and they had three small daughters and a son when they purchased the hotel. As Mary described it, "When we bought it the building was almost an empty shell, but for a large kitchen range, oak player piano, oak roll-top desk, and some beds. The saloon had the usual fixtures and billiard tables (and lovely crystal glass mirrors). There was also a library."[24] The Green Lantern Hotel had been built with gas lighting, and the new owners' first order of business was to install a generator to produce heat and electric lighting.

The Crucils owned and operated the Green Lantern Hotel until 1943. During that time, the bar and dining room catered to longshoremen, loggers, salesmen, the occasional sawmill worker (most workers who built the new sawmill ate and drank at the Horseshoe Bay Hotel), and tourists who arrived by train and by automobile. Following the Crucils as owners were W.J. Drummon and J. Foley, who ran the historic hotel for a few years before it changed ownership yet again, and a parade of owners came and went after that.

Meanwhile, after selling the hotel, the Crucil family settled in Chemainus. In 1946, their only son, eighteen-year-old Karl Matthew, was killed when working in the woods. That tragic event was followed two years later by a logging accident on Mount Sicker that claimed Frank Crucil's life.[25]

ABBOTSFORD HOTEL
1894—1935

It was a seven-mile train journey northwest from Chemainus Station to Ladysmith, with a brief stop at Blainey's train station at approximately the halfway mark. As the train wound through patches of farmland interspersed with old-growth forest, travellers

Abbotsford Hotel, Ladysmith, British Columbia,
Proprietor—A. J. McMURTRIE.

Above: The Abbotsford Hotel was built in the mining town of Wellington in 1894, prior to its move to Ladysmith in 1900. Image 2007-034-073 courtesy of the Ladysmith and District Archives.

Left: The Abbotsford Hotel at its new home in Ladysmith. Originally built in Wellington, the Abbotsford Hotel was cut into sections and placed on E&N flat cars and moved to Ladysmith when the coal ran out. Postcard from the author's collection.

occasionally had good views of the Strait of Georgia from the east-facing windows. Before long, the train slowed and came to a stop at Ladysmith Station.

The town of Ladysmith could have easily been called Dunsmuirville, for it was James Dunsmuir, the son of coal baron and original E&N owner Robert Dunsmuir, who founded Ladysmith in 1900. The town came into existence with the help of Mother Nature, as it was blessed with a deep-sea port at Oyster Bay, and this attracted Dunsmuir to choose it as a holding pen for coal from his mines in Wellington and Extension before it was loaded onto waiting ships. Ladysmith became the bedroom community for the coal facilities at Oyster Bay. By 1901, the coal mines at Extension were at full production, extracting several hundred thousand tons of coal to be shipped out to local and American markets each year, and Ladysmith became the key transportation hub.[26]

But back in 1900, despite having a few rough dirt roads leading north and south, Ladysmith was an isolated community, and the importance of the E&N Railway link cannot be overstressed. The railroad brought settlers, day trippers, salespeople, freight, and news, all of which helped grow the economy. The train station was the hub of the young community, with trains arriving and departing twice daily in clouds of smoke and steam, the train whistle and bell like music to the ears of local residents.[27]

Upon arriving at Ladysmith within a few months of its 1900 founding, E&N passengers would have witnessed a veritable beehive of activity as buildings of all sorts were rapidly being erected. Some of the finest hotels and stores to be found anywhere outside of the larger cities were opening in Ladysmith, even though the town was not yet five months old.

Among the new structures in Ladysmith was the thirty-room Abbotsford Hotel, one of the town's earliest hotels.[28] But in fact the Abbotsford was not new at all. Originally built in 1894 in the village of Wellington, a booming coal mining town between Ladysmith and Nanaimo, the Abbotsford Hotel had been cut into pieces and moved from Wellington to Ladysmith by train, then reassembled in Dunsmuir's new town.

In the years before Dunsmuir founded Ladysmith, Wellington had been the major coal-mining centre in the region, and among the shrewd businessmen who came to make their fortunes there was Andrew J. McMurtrie, from Ayrshire, Scotland. In November 1893, McMurtrie had joined with J.A. Thompson, E. Patten, and R. McManusin and started the Wellington Investment and Improvement Company, with a capital of $200,000. "The company was organized for the purposes of erecting a hotel, theatre, brewery, and other buildings on the new townsite of Wellington, and to engage in such industries as the shareholders may consider fit and proper."[29] Within six months, McMurtrie and company had built the ornate Abbotsford Hotel on the main street of Wellington.

McMurtrie liked politics, and in January 1898 he was elected mayor of Wellington, receiving forty-six out of a possible eighty-two votes.[30] The following year, the village of Wellington purchased a new steam fire engine, and after it passed a number of tests, the mayor invited guests to a banquet at his hotel. After consuming a delicious meal and copious amounts of drink, it was decided to name the new fire engine after the popular Mayor McMurtrie.[31] There aren't many people who have a fire truck named after them!

But the death knell for the town of Wellington came in 1900, when the coal seam was played out. James Dunsmuir forced the townsfolk to either move to Ladysmith, his new town at Oyster Bay, or remain unemployed in Wellington. A few people did choose the latter, but most packed all they had and moved—including McMurtrie and his thirty-room Abbotsford Hotel.

Now situated in Ladysmith on Esplanade Street next door to the Grand Hotel and just a short walk to the E&N Railway station, the Abbotsford underwent a number of quick updates to its guest rooms, dining room, and hotel bar before getting back into business in a jiffy.

By 1904, fifteen hotels were competing for guests in Ladysmith. The economy was booming as the mines kept producing and shipping their black gold to be processed at the docks in Ladysmith. The McMurtries had two healthy sons, Ian and John, and McMurtrie was as involved in his community as ever, an active member of the Ancient Order of the Free Masons and past vice president of the Wellington Bicycle Club.[32] He was also asked if he would run for mayor of Ladysmith, but he declined—perhaps because his business was doing so well.[33] Hotel rooms and hotel bars were packed, and the sale of beer and spirits was a substantial business in the growing town.[34]

Many hotel guests worked in the mines and were either waiting for their homes to be built or were transient single men considering their future. During their downtime, a group of boarders staying at the Abbotsford Hotel once issued a challenge to every other hotel in town to assemble a team to compete in any sport, from ping-pong to marbles.[35]

In 1908, an incident took place in the kitchen of the Abbotsford Hotel that made the newspapers when the case went to court. When McMurtrie asked Joe, the hotel's general utility man, to tell the dishwasher he was not doing his job properly, Joe did as requested. The dishwasher, however, did not take the news well, and a confrontation quickly ensued in which Joe slapped the dishwasher and the dishwasher hit Joe on the head with a potato squeezer, slashed Joe's arm three times, and pinned him to the floor. In the end, the dishwasher was fined twenty dollars.[36]

A more serious problem arose at the hotel in March 1909, when a rumour presented as fact was published in the local newspaper claiming that the Abbotsford Hotel was closed under quarantine. The rumour proved incorrect, and the newspaper issued a quick retraction, but business at the Abbotsford fell off for a short while.

In October 1909, a terrible explosion occurred at one of the Extension mines killing thirty-two miners. Most of the miners who died had lived in Ladysmith.[37]

In August 1912, the Canadian army set up a camp outside the Abbotsford Hotel. The camp housed 130 soldiers sent to Ladysmith to impede the Great Strike in the Dunsmuir mines and to maintain the peace. James Dunsmuir was ruthless in his handling of the strikers, and he would use any means to put down the strike. "It was a very hard road for the average Dunsmuir employee, especially in the mines. The threat of immediate eviction from the company-owned houses helped keep 'the workers in line' But strikes did take place: 1877, 1883, 1890–1891, and the Big Strike of 1912–1914 in which the army was called in to quell the strikers."[38]

The Abbotsford Hotel sketched by Marianne Torkko, 1976. Image from author's collection.

Fast-forward to 1931, and we see that McMurtrie was still running the Abbotsford Hotel. The mines at Extension closed that year, in part because the coal seams were almost played out, but more importantly because petroleum, a cheaper (at the time) and more plentiful energy source, was increasingly replacing bulky and dirty coal.[39] As the coal mines closed, other industries, especially logging, filled the gap and kept the economy going. The transition was slow and difficult for many, but the town survived.

Just as the economy was shifting from coal to lumber, the fortunes of the Abbotsford Hotel shifted too. On January 4, 1935, McMurtrie died at the age of seventy-three.[40] His distinctive Abbotsford Hotel was sold in the estate sale to the City of Ladysmith. It languished for a few years before the Comox Logging and Railway Company bought it and converted it into a boarding house for employees.[41] It was used for that purpose until 1959, then demolished in 1968—a regrettable loss of a piece of Ladysmith history.[42]

CASSIDY
MILE 105

PARKSVILLE
MILE 153

CHAPTER 5
Cassidy to Parksville

PASSENGERS ON THE E&N LINE heading north from Ladysmith crossed the flat farmlands from Brenton to Granby in the Nanaimo Regional District. Located south of Nanaimo in a rural area, Granby was the original settlement in what is now known as Cassidy, home to the Raymond Collishaw Air Terminal, Nanaimo's only airfield.

The community took root in 1914, when the Granby Consolidated Mining, Smelting, and Power Company sent their surveyors and engineers to an isolated area between Nanaimo and Ladysmith after a large coal seam was discovered. The Douglas coal seam appeared to have an endless supply of high-grade coal, and the company began laying out a townsite that they named Granby.

Extraction of coal began in 1918, and the town of Granby grew up around it. Connected to the E&N Railway by a three-mile spur line, the town proved a popular choice for coal miners to live and work due to the higher wages paid by the company and the new and attractive townsite.[1] Covering one hundred acres, Granby included fifty residential houses of various sizes; a department store and theatre; modern water, sewer, and power systems; and paved, tree-lined streets with sidewalks and boulevards. There was also a single-men's dormitory built of cement to accommodate workers in seventy-six rooms, all with separate entrances, light, hot and cold water, and steam heat.

Also among the buildings was a bunkhouse and reception centre for surveyors and engineers—the same building that ultimately became the Cassidy Hotel.

Cassidy Inn, ca. 1980, from a sketch by Jaki Makokis. Image from author's collection.

CASSIDY HOTEL
1914 — 2016

During the years 1921–22, with its mine at peak production, the Granby Consolidated Mining, Smelting, and Power Company employed 450 men, most of whom lived in the company-built town.[2] When the townsfolk asked for a recreation centre, the company repurposed the bunkhouse, added a store, and hired experienced storekeeper Napoleon Manca to run it. Manca had owned a wholesale liquor outfit in Ladysmith back in 1908.[3]

Business was so good that Manca expanded the size of his store, and in 1925, he added the Cassidy Hotel and was granted a beer parlour licence. By 1928, the town had a population of just over five hundred, two hundred of whom worked in the mines. The town of Granby changed its name to Cassidy in honour of Thomas Cassidy, who had pioneered the area in the 1870s.

By 1932, the Douglas coal seam was mined out, and worldwide demand for coal had fallen in favour of other resources, such as oil. The Granby mine at Cassidy closed at the height of the Great Depression, and the promising town of Cassidy almost died with it. In 1936, the mining company auctioned off everything that couldn't be moved away, and only a handful of residents and businesses remained—including Manca and his Cassidy Hotel.

Even with fewer customers on his immediate doorstep, Manca thought of creative ways to attract them inside. For example, he found a charming old player piano that he just had to have. The magnificent seven-foot, 1,500-pound piano had a painting of a buxom woman, typical of the framed pictures often seen above saloon bars. Built in Brussels in 1890 by an Italian maker, the piano had travelled by steamship, train, and finally dogsled to a wealthy owner in Dawson City, who paid the princely sum of $1,850, before finding its way to Manca's Cassidy Hotel. To operate the piano, one would put a coin (a small nickel in those days) into a slot, choose one of ten delightful tunes, then crank the large handle to start the music.

Although Manca hoped to have the piano refurbished for his beer parlour, the law at the time forbade music and entertainment of any kind, so it sat neglected in a back storage room for years, likely put to use only from 1954 onward, when the strict rules governing beer parlours were relaxed.[4] And it sure needed tuning! "Old timers still ask occasionally for the old player piano that used to sit in the pub."[5, 6]

In 1947, Manca sold the Cassidy Hotel to a Mr. Hodge, who updated and renovated the hotel, added more rooms, and enlarged the popular beer parlour. In 1953, Hodge sold it to the Osbornes; the hotel and the beer parlour, in particular, continued to be profitable, and business prospects increased when the nearby portion of the Island Highway was widened and finally paved in 1953, allowing for an increase in traffic and more business for the hotel and bar from Nanaimo and points south.

By the 1970s, however, the place was looking pretty rough (rustic, some may say), although I loved the look and feel of the place—good service, cheap beer, and very laid-back. In January 1983, owners Jane and Bob Kelly revived the waning Cassidy Inn, as it was then known, as a neighbourhood pub. They operated it until Harry Ahokas arrived from Finland and bought the place in 1989.[7] The Cassidy Inn had great live country and western music. Saturday afternoons beginning at three, the c&w jam started—a real draw for those of all generations (over the age of 19). Food was also much improved during these years. The Cassidy turned into a terrific neighbourhood pub.

In the 1990s Vic Charlton purchased the charming Cassidy Inn where he continued the music mixed with motorcycles. "As befits a longstanding local landmark, The Cassidy Inn is comfortably old-fashioned. Its homey, sometimes smoky interior—including those terry cloth covers on the tables—recalls its half-century of service as one of the few roadhouses on the route between Victoria and Nanaimo."[8] But the smoking bylaw and later the strict drinking-and-driving legislation, coupled with the tragic accident and potential for more accidents when the Island Highway was widened and the Cassidy Inn was on its edge; all these factors eventually led to its closing in 2012.

The old Inn sat vacant and neglected for a number of years as the last owner, Manno Pawar, contemplated what to do with the historic pub. The Cassidy Inn's last days saw squatters occasionally staying in the empty building and its final dramatic end came in a ball of fire on the evening of July 4, 2016.

ROYAL HOTEL
1878 – 1894

From Cassidy it was a short train trip north to the city of Nanaimo. In an 1890 letter to the editor of the *Daily Colonist*, Mrs. Little described her experience when arriving in Nanaimo for the first time on the E&N passenger train: "Nanaimo is singularly blessed by nature as to position, but the smells there are at present so distressing, that one hesitates to recommend the tourist to remain there for one night."[9] Such were the smells of progress.

This was coal country and had been since the Hudson's Bay Company (HBC) began coal-mining operations in 1852, after an Indigenous person found a lump of coal on the surface of what turned out to be a large outcrop of high-quality, bituminous coal above the highwater mark near what is today Front Street in downtown Nanaimo.[10]

A small community soon sprang up around the newly discovered coal seam on the shore of Wentuhuysen Inlet (now called Nanaimo Harbour). The area was known to Indigenous peoples as *Syn-ny-mo*, but the HBC initially called it Colville after Andrew Colville, governor of the HBC at the time. In 1860, the name changed from Colville to Nanaimo.

Coal was the main economic engine for the growing community, and along with the coal mines came the businesses essential in every boomtown, including hotels—though not everyone welcomed these establishments. In the spring of 1874, Mark Bate, Nanaimo's first mayor, wrote, "The town continues to grow and many new buildings are going up, some of them not wanted. I allude to the two new hotels. When those two are finished we shall have no less than six drinking places in a line within a distance of 450 yards, Licenses granted by Capt. Spalding without any regard to the wants of the place, and it seems a great pity that there should be so many inducements put in men's way to drink. It is a great drawback to workers, and an injury to the community generally."[11]

One of the hotels Bate was referring to was the Royal Hotel, built by Richard Watkins in 1878 on the corner of Wharf and Commercial Streets in downtown Nanaimo—the site formerly

Facing page, top to bottom: Brechin No. 4 Mine (New Northfield), Nanaimo, owned by the Western Fuel Company from 1903-14. This postcard was mailed in 1909. Image from author's collection; Nanaimo was built on coal. Photograph by the author.

Coal Co.'s Wharves, Nanaimo, British Columbia.

NO.1 MINE

Nanaimo was founded as a coal-mining settlement in 1852. Its most productive mine, No. 1, opened in 1881. From the bottom of the main shaft, one-half mile south of here, a labyrinth of workings extended for miles under the sea. These operations were served also by a shaft on Protection Island at the harbour's entrance. Until No. 1 closed in 1938, it was the oldest operating mine in the province.

PROVINCE OF
BRITISH COLUMBIA
19 66

The Royal Hotel, where Prime Minister John A. Macdonald stayed when driving the last stake opening the E&N railway in 1886. Image C3-2 courtesy of the Nanaimo Museum.

occupied by the What Cheer House, which had burned down the previous year. The two-storey wooden Royal Hotel offered the obligatory bar and nicely fitted rooms, but it also had a barber shop and a popular restaurant employing a "first-class French cook."[12] Next door to the hotel was the fire hall, which must have provided some comfort for hotel guests in the days when fire destroyed wooden buildings with alarming regularity.

Perhaps one of the most significant events to take place at the short-lived Royal Hotel occurred when Sir John A. Macdonald and his entourage stayed there in the summer of 1886 after hammering in the last spike of the E&N Railway at Cliffside, near Shawnigan Lake. In a photograph from the time, Macdonald can be seen pacing and taking in the view from the hotel's handsome wraparound veranda.[13] After the ceremony, the group travelled by train to Nanaimo, where a reception and banquet was held at the Royal Hotel. The group of dignitaries included Prime Minister and Lady Macdonald, Mayor Bate, city council members, and the E&N's smiling founder, Robert Dunsmuir, who invited Prime Minister and

Lady Macdonald to Shed No. 1 inside one of Dunsmuir's coal mines to continue the celebrations of the momentous occasion. He also remembered to bring with him an ample supply of strong Scotch whisky. The ladies in the group wisely declined the invitation to join the men deep in the bowels of the Dunsmuir mine.

The Royal Hotel's proprietor, Watkins, was an avid fisherman who enjoyed days on the nearby Chase River and on frequent trips to more distant waters. He also enjoyed organizing raffles and betting on various events. On August 23, 1889, a 190-yard footrace between two of the most sure-footed men in the city was organized by employee George McAllister of the Royal Hotel. The winner received a seventy-five-dollar prize, but it was the side bets that made people money, as the race was well advertised and drew a substantial crowd.[14]

In September 1889, Watkins completely renovated the Royal Hotel, bringing the plumbing, lighting system, and decor up to date for prospective guests.[15] Not long after, in 1892, Watkins sold the hotel to David H. Adams. (Watkins's name lives on in south Nanaimo, where a street was named in his honour; Watkins Street runs west to east off of Victoria Road, between Needham and Pine Streets, ending before reaching the Trans-Canada Highway.)

The Royal's new owner, Adams, also dabbled in local politics; in the 1894 civic elections, his name was removed from the list of candidates because he had neglected to give an address for his residence as required. Despite this setback to his political career, he left the hotel business that same year. Joseph Cuffolo took over from Adams as the third proprietor of the Royal Hotel—and unfortunately its last.[16]

At approximately five o'clock in the morning of September 28, 1894, the bane of all wooden structures struck at the Royal Hotel when fire and smoke were reported coming from the second floor. The two-storey wood structure was tinder dry from a long, hot summer, and it provided the perfect fuel for the hungry flames that rapidly consumed the hotel. There were nineteen people in the hotel at the time of the fire, including four women, and they ran and jumped for their lives in order to escape. Multiple injuries resulted, especially for people who had no other means of escape but to jump from windows at the rear of the hotel into the dark water-filled ravine below. Adjoining buildings were soon ablaze as well, and business after business fell like dominoes as the fast-moving fire burned everything in its path, including the old fire station. If it had not been for the sustained and heroic efforts of firefighters and dozens of citizens, the loss of life and destruction of property would have been much worse.[17]

When the fire was finally under control, it took hours to extinguish the remaining hot spots and begin assessing damages. Initially it was believed that two people had died in the blaze—an Irishman named Patrick McGee and the Royal Hotel bartender, Fritz, but it was later determined that McGee was the only fatality.[18] After spending the previous evening drinking in the Royal Hotel bar, the retired bootblack from Belfast had gone to bed about two in the morning and had evidently not heard the shouts to evacuate.[19]

Three other people were badly burned, and a fourth, Miss Minnie Corcoran, suffered a broken back after jumping out a rear window and falling awkwardly into the ravine. The fire was deemed suspicious, and talk that it may have been set deliberately was in the news and on the lips of most everyone for the next several days. The outrage of local voters motivated Nanaimo City Council to amend bylaws in order to provide better fire protection for citizens, such as requiring that buildings be equipped with an adequate number of fire escapes to avoid such a tragic event in the future.[20]

Ten months after the fire, on July 16, 1895, Miss Corcoran was released from the hospital in a wheelchair and was expected to recover from the ordeal.[21]

Like the What Cheer House before it, the Royal Hotel was completely destroyed by the fire and was never rebuilt. Joe Cuffolo subsequently opened the Royal Saloon at 32 Finlayson Street, but there is no record of its existence after 1895.

OCCIDENTAL HOTEL

SINCE 1887

The 1880s saw a marked increase in the
number of new hotels in Nanaimo, and
Samuel Fiddick's handsome and imposing

Samuel Fiddick, owner of
the Occidental Hotel, in
Nanaimo, 1895. Image
I1-31 courtesy of the
Nanaimo Museum.

two-storey brick Occidental Hotel was one of the best. Built in
1886 and opening to much fanfare and flag-waving on February
7, 1887, the new brick railroad hotel was designed by renowned
architect John Teague in the Victorian Italianate style popular in

North America at the time. Although most of the 350 buildings Teague designed in his long and successful career were in his native Victoria, it was fitting that this eldest son of a tin and copper mine agent should design a hotel in a busy coal-mining centre like Nanaimo. He also designed the Masonic Lodge in town.[22]

Built at a cost of $8,000, the Occidental Hotel dominated the corner of Selby and Fitzwilliam Streets, just a beer-bottle-cap toss away from the E&N train station. Fiddick had intentionally built his hotel in close proximity to the station to attract potential guests arriving by train. In fact, the hotel received the nickname "the first and last," because it was the first hotel nearest to the train station for arrivals and the last hotel for those departing by train to points north or south along the E&N line.

The Occidental reflected the optimism and prosperity that was prevalent at the time, due not only to the completion of the E&N Railway, but also to the expansion of the huge No. 1 Coal Mine.[23] Every room was quickly booked up, and it remained very popular with the travelling public for years. It consisted of a billiards room in the bar, a spacious dining room, and a wide hall ending in a staircase that led to thirteen rooms on the second floor.[24]

Fiddick was a tin smith in Cornwall, England, when, in 1854, he crossed the Atlantic to work as a miner for the Hudson's Bay Company on Newcastle Island. Fiddick and fellow miner John Bryant, also from Cornwall, tried their luck in the goldfields of the Fraser River and the Cariboo, but they returned to Vancouver Island after an unfruitful attempt at striking it rich.[25] Fiddick's dream of finding gold remained elusive, though he never stopped trying. The man proved lucky in another way, though, when in April 1863, he met Elizabeth Grandam from Tynemouth, Northumberland, England. They married shortly after, and in subsequent years, they had ten children together.

Fiddick continued to dabble in gold prospecting on Vancouver Island, and in 1884, his efforts finally paid off when he and partner James Beck sold the mineral rights of five hundred acres they owned along the Nanaimo River to Dunsmuir and Sons for the reported amount of $40,000. The windfall helped Fiddick pay for his handsome new hotel three years later.

Fiddick had itchy feet, and within six months of opening the Occidental Hotel, he put it up for lease: "Hotel to Rent—Proposals are invited immediately for the leasing of the commodious Occidental Hotel, adjoining the depot of the E&N railway in the City of Nanaimo. This hotel is a fire proof brick building, two stories in height, and furnished throughout with all the modern appliances and conveniences."[26] Now in his sixties, Fiddick planned for one more trip to the Interior to prospect for gold, but it is unclear if he acted on this impulse. In the winter of 1888, Fiddick's son and namesake, Samuel, caught a severe cold while out hunting. He neglected to seek treatment and soon developed diphtheria, which took his life. He was only seventeen years old.[27]

In February 1889, Fiddick finally leased the Occidental Hotel to John Decker and a silent partner named Weldon who worked as a conductor for the E&N Railway. Decker brought enthusiasm and fresh ideas to the elegant and commodious Occidental. He launched an extensive advertising campaign to attract customers, especially passengers on the E&N train. His ads ran daily in a number of Vancouver Island papers from March through August 1889. And although the hotel was only two years old, Decker and company completed a series of renovations to fit the hotel with the finest and most up-to-date facilities at the time. They expanded and improved the hotel bar and provided not only the usual large selection of wines, liquors, cigars, and beers, but added the celebrated Wieland's Philadelphia Lager Beer on draft. Upon completion of the renovations, the Occidental was truly a first-class railroad hotel.[28]

The partners leased the Occidental Hotel for five successful years. When their lease expired in 1894, S. (Gus) Steffen took over as leaseholder. Steffen then sold the lease to J.B. Ward, who ran the Occidental from 1897 to 1899.

From top: A postcard depicting the colourful Occidental Hotel, now a three-storey structure, ca. 1968. Image from the author's collection; A contemporary photograph of the Occidental (Oxy) Pub taken by the author in August 2015. Note the building had been renovated back to its original two-storey configuration.

Fiddick continued to lease out the hotel until his death on January 9, 1900, at the age of sixty-seven. Among the pallbearers at his well-attended funeral were his old friends John Bryant and Mayor Mark Bate. After Fiddick's passing, the Occidental Hotel stayed in the family until it was sold in 1906. (Widow Elizabeth Fiddick survived her husband by twenty-eight years until she died at the respectable age of eighty-four. Seven of their ten children survived her passing, and most of the offspring lived in the Nanaimo area.)

After leaving the hands of the Fiddick family, the Occidental Hotel went through six different proprietors until James (Jim) Handelin (there are various spellings of his surname) brought some stability to the place—though it was during Handelin's tenure that John Aitken of nearby Selby Street was stabbed just outside the Occidental Hotel in 1912. The perpetrator, Robert Longmate, was arrested near the scene of the crime.[29] It is unknown if the confrontation had anything to do with the hotel or the hotel bar, but such assaults and public drunkenness were an unfortunately common part of the culture of the times.

In October 1917, Prohibition closed the bar, but the hotel continued to operate under the proprietorship of J. Clovis. In 1920, Antonio (Tony) and Alice Gallia purchased the hotel, and in March 1925, they applied for a beer parlour licence. When they were told that the hotel had to have a minimum of thirty-two rooms to be granted a liquor licence, they added a third floor. The Occidental Hotel was a three-storey structure for the next sixty-four years, until the upper floor was removed in 1989 and the appearance of the historic building returned to its original two-storey configuration.

The Occidental Hotel, now referred to as the Oxy Pub, continues to serve quality food and beverages to its customers. Stepping into the pub is like stepping into the past, with very few changes to the interior since the hotel first opened. Other than stucco covering the original brick and a few "artistic" additions, the exterior is also relatively unchanged from its original appearance. The building is the oldest-surviving pub in Nanaimo and is listed on the Canadian

PARKSVILLE, V.I.

Registry of Historic Places.[30] It is also my favourite pub in town and now my local. I hope this landmark historical building continues to operate successfully for many more years to come.

The Rod & Gun was originally the Sea View Hotel, as shown here, ca. 1890. Image E01880 courtesy of the Royal BC Museum and Archives.

ROD & GUN HOTEL

SINCE 1895

In 1910, the E&N Railway arrived in Parksville, twenty-four miles northwest of Nanaimo on the Strait of Georgia, bringing prosperity and a boost of optimism to the growing community.[31] "Parksville is experiencing an era of unbounded prosperity and now has the appearance of a prosperous village.... Included in the new buildings recently erected is an addition to the Rod and Gun Hotel, which will involve an expenditure of $4,000 or more," read the local newspaper a few years after the E&N's arrival.[32]

The Rod & Gun, owned by the Hirst family, actually had its roots in a hotel first established by the family in 1886, the same year that a wagon road was completed connecting Parksville (then called McBride) to Nanaimo. The Hirsts' history in the area went back even further. John Hirst, a businessman from Nanaimo, was the first person to purchase land in the area when, in 1873, he secured three hundred acres on both sides of the Englishman River.[33] When John Hirst died in 1882, the land was willed, in parcels, to his six sons. Albert was the first of the Hirst brothers to settle on the property in 1883.

In 1886, the new wagon road was bringing more settlers and visitors to the area. John Hirst, Jr., who already operated a store there, opened a hotel beside it. Hirst originally called the hotel the Sea View. John and his wife, Ann (née Harris), welcomed their son, Thomas, in 1887, the same year the name of the community changed to Parksville. By 1889, the boundary of the tiny community of thirty-eight people was extended from Englishman River to French Creek, and a second hotel—the Arlington, operated by Mrs. Belyea—gave Hirst some competition.

The 1890s brought a series of changes for the large Hirst family. Andrew, the youngest of the Hirst brothers, was appointed postmaster of Parksville in 1892; his brother Thomas died in Nanaimo the following year. Then, in 1894, the Sea View Hotel burned to the ground. John Hirst, Jr. built a new hotel in 1895—the present Rod & Gun—on a new piece of land purchased from Nelson Parks.

"In its hey-day, [the Rod & Gun] was the headquarters of various political parties and the meeting place of the district."[34] But Hirst didn't get to enjoy his new and popular hotel for long. He was found dead in October 1897 from an apparent suicide. He had ingested a lethal dose of carbolic acid and had suffered a rather painful and gruesome death.[35] His wife, thirty-two-year-old Ann, was left behind with five children, but Mrs. Hirst proved to be a strong and resourceful woman. Within three years of her husband's death, Ann had a new post and telegraph office built near the Rod & Gun, and she served as both postmistress and hotelier until selling the hotel to the Cook family in 1918, after Prohibition came into effect.[36]

On the heels of the E&N coming to town in 1910, the advent of the automobile also began to make an impact on the landscape. The rise of the automobile brought with it the "auto court" and a new and personal way of getting around and touring Vancouver Island. Once the word got out about the fantastic beaches of Parksville and Qualicum Beach, the area saw a sharp increase of holiday visitors. Every summer, more vacationers arrived in the area, and more auto courts and hotels were built to accommodate them. "Excellent beaches combined with the summer sun attracted day trippers and holiday seekers to the region . . . many tourists coming back to the same resort."[37] The E&N tried to compete by offering cut-rate excursions and holiday packages each season to Parksville–Qualicum and Shawnigan Lake.[38]

The Rod & Gun Hotel continued on as a successful business through the Prohibition years and into the 1920s. In March 1925, the owners applied for and were granted a beer parlour licence.

The Rod & Gun and the train station are the oldest buildings in Parksville today, with the hotel building still standing on the corner of the Alberni Highway and, quite fittingly, Hirst Avenue. Now operating as the Rod & Gun Restaurant and Bar, it is open seven days a week, has 160 seats in the pub and 30 on a patio, and offers live music most nights.[39]

Above: A contemporary view of the
Rod & Gun Hotel, 2005. Photo by
the author.

Left: The original safe used at the Rod
& Gun. It is no longer in use and is
decorated and displayed in the pub.
Photo by the author.

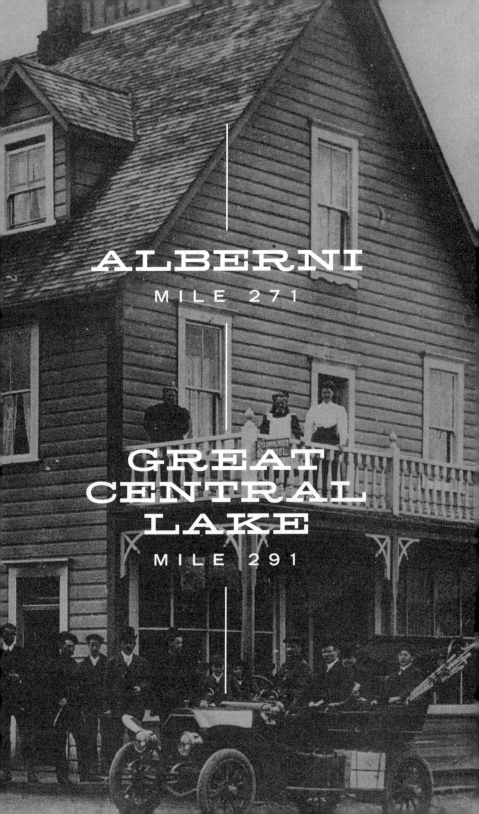

ALBERNI

MILE 271

GREAT CENTRAL LAKE

MILE 291

CHAPTER 6
Alberni to Great Central Lake

TRAVELLING FROM PARKSVILLE ON THE
E&N, one had the choice to continue north
or to travel west along the Alberni subdivision to Cameron Lake; then it continued
on along the western slopes of the Beaufort
range to the Alberni Valley.

E&N Railway train arriving
in the Alberni Valley,
December 1911. Alberni
Valley Museum Photograph
Collection PN00558.

The Alberni subdivision was one of a series of branches off the
main E&N line that the Canadian Pacific Railway (CPR) constructed
after purchasing the E&N from James Dunsmuir in 1905, and it

proved to be one of the biggest challenges since the Malahat. In 1906, a preliminary survey from Wellington to Alberni began with provincial land surveyor Frank Sheppard in charge. It took a year to complete before the final route was chosen. Shovels went into the ground in 1907, and it was relatively easy going to Cameron Lake. From there the section up and over the Arrowsmith summit proved to be the most challenging of all. It took four years before the first E&N train would travel the thirty-eight miles from Parksville to the train station at New Alberni (Port Alberni).[1]

The arrival of the E&N in the twin cities of Alberni and Port Alberni had a profound positive effect on the communities, just as it did for other communities on Vancouver Island, and among the beneficiaries were three pioneer hotels: the Arlington Hotel, the Somass Hotel, and the Ark Resort.

ARLINGTON HOTEL

SINCE 1893

Opening in the spring of 1893, the Arlington Hotel was the second hotel in the tiny settlement of Alberni, preceded in 1892 by the Alberni Hotel located a few blocks to the northwest. Built by Mathew A. Ward on the southwest corner of Johnston Road and Margaret Street during the Alberni mining boom, the three-storey Arlington "boasted a large veranda on the front and four dormers on each side of the top floor. It included a dining room that seated 90 people and a modern saloon."[2] Lanterns strung along a rope handrail led the way to the dining room.

The Arlington Hotel became very popular, "the best-known house on the West Coast of Vancouver Island."[3] Ward proved to be a genial host, providing comfortable rooms for his guests, organizing excellent banquets for various social groups and clubs (including the IOF, Independent Order of Foresters [4]), and providing a coach in the early years and later an Oldsmobile to pick up and drop off hotel guests at the train station. Fully stocked with the

The original Arlington Hotel in Alberni, ca. 1908. Image courtesy of the Alberni Valley Museum Photograph Collection PN00688.

best cigars and liquors, the hotel's saloon did a roaring business, as did the Alberni Hotel Saloon just a short distance away. Both were located in the centre of town, and both served as social hubs for the entire Alberni Valley. Even before the Arlington Hotel was completed, the community held square dances on its newly finished dance floor. Couples circled and whirled in two-steps and waltzes to music provided by Mrs. Ward on the piano.[5]

The Arlington Hotel provided a good living for Ward and his family, but Ward was an enterprising man. In addition to owning the hotel, he was a partner in the Hetty Green Mines on Deer Creek in Alberni, which showed signs of being a valuable producer in the near future. Mining was an important industry in the

Alberni Valley in the early years of the town's development, and by the 1910s, the valley was fast becoming a tourist destination as well, especially with the arrival of the E&N train in 1911 making the long journey there much easier.

In July 1912, Ward sold the hotel to James A. McNiff and O.H. Meagher (Ward retired to Victoria, where he died in 1916, leaving a wife, two sons, and a daughter). The new owners were eager to expand the hotel, and in September 1912, work began to enlarge existing rooms and add several stories to the original structure. By December, McNiff and Meagher also had electric lights installed, and a private electric light plant on the premises that not only served to light the inside of the hotel but also threw a searchlight up Johnston Road, guiding incoming tourists to the hotel. A gas generator was added in December 1912, and that powered coloured lights in the dining room.

The newly renovated and expanded Arlington Hotel reopened to an appreciative public in September 1913. "Hotel Arlington, the old and ever popular headquarters for the High-class Island trade has recently been greatly enlarged and now contains sixty rooms, single or en suite," the *Alberni Advocate* reported. "The splendid new dining room contains a fine selection of island views from the studio of Mr. Leonard Frank."[6]

McNiff and Meagher continued the first-class service begun by Ward, hosting various functions in the hotel, such as bachelors' dances and grand masquerade balls complete with a full orchestra; gentlemen (masked) entered for $1.60, ladies (masked) were free, and spectators entered for fifty cents.[7]

The years 1910–13 brought an economic boom both to the Alberni Valley and British Columbia in general. Industry was very productive, unemployment was low, and the logging and sawmill industry was at its peak. Everyone was doing well, including the hotels. But as is the case in a boom and bust economy, a downward trend in the market suddenly brought the good times to an end. In 1914, just prior to the outbreak of the First World War, the

Arlington Hotel, like many businesses in the Alberni Valley, fell on hard times.

On October 15, 1915, McNiff appeared before the liquor board on behalf of the Arlington and Alberni hotels, asking for a temporary reduction of the liquor licence fees and arguing that the hotels would likely go out of business if the fees were not lowered in these difficult economic times. His request was turned down, and the Alberni Hotel did indeed close.

Arlington Hotel, 1913, Leonard Frank photograph. Image courtesy of the Alberni Valley Museum Photograph Collection PN00319.

Although the Arlington Hotel carried on, another major challenge to keep its doors open came into effect on October 1, 1917, when the Prohibition Act closed the hotel bar and dried up a major revenue source. Despite these setbacks, the hotel remained open, in part due to its importance as the social hub of Alberni. The hotel continued to hold dances and provide meeting rooms for local societies and clubs, hotel rooms continued to be booked, and the restaurant survived.

In 1925, the BC government started issuing beer parlour licences, and the Arlington Hotel was among the applicants in the Alberni Valley (along with the Somass, King Edward, and Beaufort hotels) first granted a licence to sell beer by the glass. A nine-ounce glass of beer sold for ten cents, and patrons had to sit to drink it. With no entertainment or food allowed, the beer parlour atmosphere was initially very spartan, but hotel owners still welcomed the reopening of their bars and the revenue they provided.

The parlours were popular with most of the public too. Local workers had just won the right for the eight-hour work day that came into effect on January 6, 1925, so when the beer parlours opened a few months later, they lined up at the doors after their shift with more free time to patronize their favourite watering hole. On any given Friday or Saturday night, the beer parlours filled to capacity with hard-working loggers, sawmill workers, fishers, farmers, and trades workers looking to blow off some steam and enjoy a drink with their friends and co-workers. All the beer parlours in town did a booming business, especially the one at the Arlington.

John (Jack) Burke, a jolly, hard-working man with a pot belly, owned the Arlington Hotel from 1925 to 1934, purchasing it from Arthur H.M. Lord. A long-time resident of Alberni and well known and respected in the community, Burke had operated the Alberni Livery Stables across the street from the Arlington Hotel, and he was working on the original paper machine for the British Columbia Pulp & Paper Manufacturing Company when he and his brother, Richard, bought the hotel.

The 1920s saw considerable changes and improvements to the liquor laws and workers' rights. In 1927, the federal government enacted the old-age pensions law, and the recipient of Canada's very first old-age pension cheque was seventy-five-year-old Alberni resident William (Bill) Henry Derby. After accepting a cheque for twenty dollars, the maximum monthly amount allowed

Bill Derby spending his pension cheque on beer in the Arlington Hotel beer parlour, 1927. Derby was the first recipient of the Old Age Pension. Image courtesy of the Alberni Valley Museum Photograph Collection PN12882.

under the Act, in a brief ceremony, Derby was later found drinking in the Arlington Hotel beer parlour, using his four newly acquired rolls of dimes for payment.[8]

In the 1930s, the Arlington Hotel changed ownership several times, first to Fred W. Austin in 1934, and then to Andy Ercolini in 1936. Ercolini operated the hotel through the war years, until 1945. Meanwhile, in 1942, new liquor laws required the separation of the sexes in beer parlours—the reasoning was that, with Canada once again at war, our fighting men had to be protected from sexually transmitted diseases, and the potentially volatile mix of women and beer was too much temptation. Owners of beer parlours had to modify or add to their existing rooms to accommodate the law, sometimes at great expense. Beer parlours were also no longer allowed to advertise, and they had to go by obscure names such as refreshment rooms or beverage rooms.

The Arlington beer parlour complied with the new law by building a new wall down the middle of the room, from the bar to the wall directly opposite; the south side was for ladies and their escorts, and the north for men only. One had to be invited to the other side of the parlour if he or she wished to drink with mixed company. This separation of the sexes continued long after the reasons for it became obsolete; it wasn't until 1964 that most beer parlours were permitted to end the segregation of the sexes. Margaret Creelman, a one-time regular customer at the Arlington beer parlour, bragged that she was the first woman to be allowed to drink with the men.[9]

The post-war years saw a number of different owners and managers come and go at the Arlington. By 1948, J.A. McBride was the manager of the hotel, which now boasted forty-eight rooms, some with and some without a bath, but all featuring new spring-filled mattresses. The rooms were modern, clean, quiet, and, of course, comfortable. Business continued to flourish well into the 1950s and 1960s.

In the early morning hours of Saturday, March 28, 1964, a series of tidal waves swept through low-lying areas of the Alberni Valley.

Triggered by an earthquake in the Gulf of Alaska, the tsunami resulted in considerable damage. The Arlington Hotel sustained only minor flooding in the basement, and its rooms and lobby soon filled to capacity with tsunami victims seeking refuge.

In subsequent decades, the old hostelry continued to do well, undergoing a number of facelifts as fashion and economics dictated. One of the more significant changes was to its name. After 119 years as the Arlington Hotel, it became the Blue Marlin Inn in 2012—though regular patrons continued to call it the Arlington. Whatever it is called, the hotel is still standing; a defiant survivor in which thousands of patrons have stayed and countless more have enjoyed a beverage or two in its saloon, beer parlour, and Arli Pub, all the while contributing to the hotel's colourful history.

SOMASS HOTEL
1896–2013

It was a short train ride south from Alberni to New Alberni,[10] where the E&N station was located within a block of the impressive Somass Hotel on the corner of Argyle and Kingsway Streets.

A hotel had been a fixture on this corner since 1896, when Victoria businessmen Chalmer and Armour built the modest two-storey Armour Hotel with finished lumber that they brought with them from Victoria on the steamship *Mischief*. New Alberni was a sea of stumps and not much else at the time, but the wharf and grocery built by Arthur E. Waterhouse of the Canadian Pacific Navigation Company a few months earlier, to accommodate the needs of the miners in the area, were signs of things to come.

By August 1, the Armour Hotel, the community's first, was open for business, and a "house-warming" party invited all in the area to attend.[11] The hotel was "without siding or paint, and contained seven sleeping rooms, dining room, kitchen and (most importantly) a saloon."[12] But unfortunately, it saw very limited business and was forced to close within a year of opening. The building sat empty

Crew building E&N tracks into Port Alberni, with the Somass Hotel in the background, 1911. Image courtesy of the Alberni Valley Museum Photograph Collection PN00156.

for over a year, while the owners waited for conditions to warrant a reopening.

In 1898, Waterhouse purchased the Armour Hotel and hired Andy Watson to manage it. A newly built wing added eight more rooms and qualified the hotel for a tavern licence. It reopened on November 30, 1898, with a new look and a new name, the New Alberni Hotel.[13] "In those days it was the place to go for an evening. All the ladies and gentlemen would get dressed up in their Sunday best."[14]

Alberni was growing thanks in part to several new mines opening in the area, and the New Alberni Hotel was "the centre of all activity as the town grew up around it."[15] The road connecting those mines to the dock went right past the hotel, and for a few years, it was the only game in town for a rest, a good meal, a game of

The Somass Hotel in 1913. Image from the author's collection.

billiards, or a drink. The alternative was a long walk or horse ride six or so miles north to the Arlington or Alberni hotels in "Old Town." A number of single men made the New Alberni Hotel their home under the care of Mrs. Watson and her sister, Mrs. "Doc" Carter.

In 1902, Waterhouse hired James (Jim) Rollings to manage the New Alberni Hotel, and one of his first acts was to change the name to the Somass and commission the design and construction of a larger hotel building behind the original, along Kingsway Avenue, that would later face the railway depot. Designed by Victoria architect George Mesher, the new four-storey Somass Hotel was magnificently crafted, with no expense spared. It loomed over the original hotel, which was converted into the hotel bar and billiards room.

In May 1906, the first automobile reached the Alberni Valley, and it was displayed in front of the Somass Hotel to a curious crowd of onlookers. Enterprising Victoria entrepreneur Bob Hutchinson was all smiles while he told the story of his adventures driving his single-cylinder, eight-horsepower Oldsmobile from Victoria to Alberni. He did it in two stages: Victoria to Nanaimo, then Nanaimo to Alberni.[16] It took him thirteen hours for the one-way journey, and it proved that automobiles could make it along the rough and at times dangerous roads.

In 1907, Waterhouse began construction of a third and final extension of the Somass Hotel that would give it an up-to-date modern look. The new three-storey, Edwardian-style building offered guests a grand view of growing Argyle Street from three sets of protruding bay windows. On July 20, 1908, Waterhouse and his new manager, Clifford Wise (who had successfully run the Cowichan Bay Hotel for a number of years), presided over the opening ceremonies. Rollings had left in 1907 to open the King Edward Hotel just up Argyle Street from the Somass. The photograph of the building of the Somass Hotel extension was found in

This photograph of workers building the Somass Hotel extension in 1907 was found inside the wall of a house being demolished on Sixth Avenue in Port Alberni and published in the *Alberni Advocate* on February 26, 1975.

Somass Hotel, Argyle Road side, 1913. Image from the author's collection.

the inner wall of a cabin being demolished on 6th Avenue in town. The cabin had belonged to Mr. Wiles, a carpenter who most likely worked building the Somass extension. The find was published in the *Alberni Advocate* newspaper on February 26, 1975.

In a 1909 *Daily Colonist* spread dedicated to the Alberni Valley, the Somass received high praise: "I stopped at the Somass Hotel, kept by Mr. Waterhouse, and found a hostelry which has been built without regard to expense or pains in order to provide a high order of comfort for its patrons."[17]

By 1910, a few local businesses began working out of the main floor of the Somass extension, such as W.D. Newcombe's realty business. The Alberni District Orchestra and Dramatic Society held their meetings at the Somass Hotel where, in October 1911, Waterhouse was elected president of the society.

In December 1911, the first E&N passenger train rolled into the Alberni Valley, and the terminus was located near the docks at the foot of Argyle Street, right across the street from the Somass Hotel. Hotel guests now had the option to visit New Alberni by boat, automobile, or train. The arrival of the first train to the twin cities of Alberni and New Alberni was a huge event attended by large, welcoming crowds at both stations. The E&N opened up the valley's markets, led to the expansion of the mills, and brought new settlers and visitors to the area and to the local hotels. Sports hunters and fishers were among those attracted to the beautiful and now more accessible Alberni Valley.

On March 12, 1912, voters in the recently incorporated town of Port Alberni went to the polls to elect the town's first councillors and mayor, a position which, when the votes were counted, went to Waterhouse. His Somass Hotel and his grocery business (the latter of which he ran with partner Mr. Green) both continued to do well, even during a worldwide recession in 1914—though there were a few setbacks. In November 1916, Miss Sarah Ann Lingard, a housekeeper at the Somass, attempted to light a fire in the fireplace using a can of coal oil. It exploded in her hand and burned her badly. She succumbed to her injuries at the West Coast General Hospital a few hours later.[18] Lingard was well respected, and the news of her death was a shock to the small community and to the staff and owners of the Somass Hotel where she had worked for the past ten years.

On a brighter note, the Avecourt Girls Club held a dinner and dance at the Somass Hotel for soldiers returning from the war in Europe in April 1917. The Somass was a popular choice for such events, and a merry time was had by all.

On the eve of Prohibition, the hotel went through a minor renovation in which four new pool tables were added and an enlarged "refreshment room" was built only to have business drop once Prohibition became law on October 1, 1917. The Somass Hotel felt the adverse effects of having its liquor sales revenue cut off, though the hotel rooms continued to fill. Mr. George Woollett was manager of the hotel at the time.[19] The barroom remained open from seven in the morning until eleven in the evening, Monday to Saturday, and closed on Sundays, but it was no longer permitted to sell anything stronger than "near beer." Patrons, especially the loggers and miners, clamoured for real beer, and it didn't take long before real beer and liquors were sold under the table in the bar. The Somass, King Edward, and Arlington hotels were each fined in police court for engaging in such activity.

Waterhouse remained the proprietor until he retired in 1939. The Somass Hotel was considered as "the hub of the fishing and hunting region unexcelled."[20] One pleasant summer evening, Waterhouse was enjoying an after-dinner aperitif and a cigar on the hotel veranda. A group of guests who had recently arrived by train were gathered on the veranda, planning the next day's hunt, when one of the men spied their host and asked if the game was as plentiful as advertised. Keeping his gaze on the nearby train station, Waterhouse pointed in that direction and said, "Does that answer your question, gentlemen?" They looked over, and to their amazement saw a large black bear sauntering leisurely along the tracks.

After forty-one years in the hotel business, Waterhouse retired in 1939. He had managed to turn the small and unprofitable Armour Hotel into a successful money-maker and had played a major role in the development of early Port Alberni. As it turns out, he left the business at just the right time.

In 1946 and 1947, two back-to-back disasters took place. On June 23, 1946, a devastating 7.3-magnitude earthquake shook Port Alberni and central Vancouver Island, causing extensive damage in Comox, Alberni, Port Alberni, and Powell River.[21] Then, on February 17, 1947, a fire—the single biggest threat to pioneer hotels made of wood—broke out in the main building of the Somass Hotel, destroying the iconic forty-five-year-old structure built along Kingsway Avenue in 1902. The fire was especially devastating as it came less than a year after extensive renovations to modernize the hotel and add fifty new rooms. Manager Ely and his family lost all their possessions to the fire.

The portion of the hotel on Argyle Street survived the fire (in fact, Woodward's held a "fire sale" in this remaining structure while its new building was under construction at Third Avenue and Marr Street in Uptown). After repairs to the Argyle Street building, new management reopened the Somass Hotel.

There are so many tales left to tell of the old hostelry, like the shenanigans of the colourful character and one-time proprietor of both the Somass and Beaufort hotels, Diamond Jim, whose exploits in local lore are legendary. But for now, the train is waiting at the station to take us on our next adventure—a visit to Great Central Lake and a floating "ark" built and operated by another important pioneer, Joe Drinkwater.[22]

ARK HOTEL

1912—1929

The small community at Great Central Lake, thirteen miles northwest of Port Alberni, initially became famous for its fishing and hunting, and it was this that prompted Joe Drinkwater, prospector, explorer, hunter, guide, and entrepreneur, to build his Ark Hotel in the area.

Originally from a large family in Brant, Ontario, where he was one of twelve siblings (eight brothers and four sister), Drinkwater first came to British Columbia in 1890. He travelled to Vancouver and then to Esquimalt, where he took up farming. Drinkwater was physically fit with an athletic build, and he possessed boundless energy. He was a jack of all trades, a capable woodsman who could build practically anything he set his mind to—he was also an accomplished photographer.

After marrying Della de la Fayette in Victoria, Drinkwater travelled with his wife to Alberni. The Drinkwaters loved the Alberni Valley and made it their home. Over the next few years, Joe poked around the area prospecting and taking photographs, and in the process, he explored much of the terrain around Sproat and Great Central Lakes. He gave the name of his wife to both Della Lake—a large lake above Great Central—and Della Falls—the spectacular falls that drained into Great Central Lake.

At the time, the only access into the region was by foot or horseback along paths created and worn by Indigenous peoples. Eventually, a rough dirt road was built to Great Central Lake, and it was the only access until the E&N spur line from Port Alberni arrived in 1925. Despite the isolation (or possibly because of it), Drinkwater and his partner Clive "Snowball" Paxton built the floating Ark Resort in 1912 for those who wanted some peace and quiet for fishing or hunting in the Great Central Lake. It was a sixteen-room floating hotel constructed entirely of red cedar. For four dollars a day or twenty-one dollars a week, each room came equipped with a bunk bed, a small table, and a heater, plus a combination dining and living room with an adjoining kitchen. Joe acted as guide while Paxton ran the boats.[23] Dinner, which was served after four PM, cost seventy-five cents and often consisted of venison or trout with blackberry pie for dessert.[24]

It didn't take long for word to get out about the fine trout and steelhead salmon fishing to be had on Great Central Lake, and about Drinkwater's floating resort. "Mr. Drinkwater, who is the old original Noah of the Central Lake Ark . . . still floats on Central Lake and has become so popular with those looking for a few days fishing that Joe had to enlarge the craft which was originally 100 feet long," reported the local newspaper in 1913.[25]

In 1919, Drinkwater purchased a gas-powered launch that could fit up to twenty-five sports fishermen at a time. With the boat, he took paying customers on Sunday excursions to the far corners of the lake, leaving from the Ark at nine-thirty in the morning and returning by six-thirty in the evening.[26] Drinkwater knew where the best fishing spots were, and most of his customers came back with a basket of fish to go with the smile on their faces. "After a day in the wet and cold the floating hotel was pure luxury, a haven of warmth and comfort," recalled one such happy guest. "In the morning . . . we tumbled from cozy beds to the kitchen to find Joe, his kettle singing, his hotcake batter mixed, thick slices of ham ready for frying and a pan of biscuits hot and crusty, lying on the oven door."[27]

In 1925, the long-anticipated E&N spur line from Port Alberni to Great Central Lake was completed. With the railroad came many changes, including the arrival of a logging company and the construction of a large sawmill, which eventually employed 160 men

Above: Postcard showing Joe Drinkwater's Ark Hotel on Great Central Lake. Leonard Frank photograph, 1912, from the author's collection.

Right: Ark Hotel collage. Image from the author's collection.

The Ark Hotel

GREAT CENTRAL LAKE.   ALBERNI, B. C.

JOE DRINKWATER, PROPRIETOR

It Is Just the Place the Sportsman Is Looking For

RATES:

Room and Board: $4.00 per Day. $21.00 per Week

Boats: $1.00 per Day.   Launches: $12.00 per Day

and around which the small community grew.[28] As part of the deal to extend the E&N to Great Central Lake, the railroad was awarded a substantial amount of land, including the shoreline around the Ark Resort.[29] Drinkwater may have not liked the changes, as he sold his floating hotel the following year to John Clark and Austin Blackburn. Three years later, the Ark Resort was destroyed by fire.

By 1929, Della Drinkwater had died. Joe retired to a comfortable cabin on the shores of Great Central Lake not far from where his famous Ark Resort was moored. Deer and bear skins covered the floors while the walls of his cabin displayed pictures of his exploits. He lived with his faithful dog, Mike, and at times he could be seen wandering the trails with Mike and a camera or fishing rod in hand.[30]

In January 1932, Joe Drinkwater was found drowned in the waters of Great Central Lake. The rugged woodsman had blazed his last trail. A few years before his death, he had built a charming cedar houseboat that he had towed to the mouth of Drinkwater and McBride Creeks. Kindness personified and the soul of hospitality, Drinkwater was fondly remembered by all who knew him and sorely missed by the hundreds of guests who had had the good fortune to stay at his hotel or fish or hunt with him as their guide.[31]

After the original Ark Hotel was destroyed by fire, John "Paddy" Burke decided to continue the tradition begun by Joe Drinkwater all those years ago and built his own version of the floating Ark Resort. When it was completed, he advertised that the Ark was back. His business proved very successful, attracting notable guests like Hollywood starlet Olivia de Havilland, who stayed with her entourage for a few days.[32] Over time, Burke added a land-based dining room, dance floor, and soda shop for the pleasure of his guests. He operated his ark until his death in 1958.

By 1971, the Ark Resort was a successful seasonal business located on the shore of Great Central Lake. Hosts Donna and Howard Ostrander offered seventeen units, trailer and camping spaces, and amenities such as flush toilets, hot and cold showers, laundry facilities, a boat ramp, moorage, and boat rentals—a far cry from the rustic yet comfortable Ark Resort that once plied the waters of Great Central Lake.

QUALICUM BEACH

MILE 164

UNION BAY

MILE 211

CHAPTER 7

Qualicum Beach to Union Bay

IN THE PIONEER YEARS, THE region from Nanoose to Qualicum–Hilliers was considered one large community.[1] Having no natural harbour and soil that was not particularly good for farming, the Parksville–Qualicum region was developed much later than most of the communities hugging the E&N line of eastern Vancouver Island. Englishman River, named for an early settler from England who drowned attempting to cross it, was the first area of European settlement in the region when Albion (Alec) Tranfield began trapping there in the 1870s and John Hirst arrived by canoe in 1873.

Loosely translated, Qualicum means "where the dog salmon run" in the Pentlatch First Nation language.[2] In 1885, Irishman John Sullivan purchased some property in what is now Coombs (named for Commissioner B. Coombs who followed years later and established a Salvation Army colony there).[3]

The E&N Railway came to Qualicum Beach in 1914, giving the small community an economic boost that helped develop the resort town. The village of Qualicum Beach was incorporated in 1942 when the population just barely topped three hundred. It is here that we meet the magnificent Money family, proprietors of the Qualicum Beach Hotel.

QUALICUM BEACH HOTEL

1913–1969

The Qualicum Beach Hotel reflected the surrounding beauty of the resort town as well as the vision of its owner, Brigadier General Noel Ernest Money, CMG, DSO, TD, and architects Karl B. Spurgin and Edmund O. Wilkins.[4] The beautiful two-storey Tudor resort hotel overlooked an eighteen-hole golf course also conceived and built by Money; its rolling greens swept down the gentle slopes toward the ocean east of the town of Qualicum Beach, allowing for spectacular views from the hotel and golf course.

Developer, visionary, hotelman, sportsman, army veteran, and devoted father: General Money was all of these things. Born in Montreal on March 17, 1867, Noel Money was the eldest son of Captain Albert William Money of the Royal Canadian Rifle Regiment. By 1871, four-year-old Noel lived in Weybridge, a suburb of London, with his two sisters. After his education at Radley and then at Christ Church, Oxford, he served in the Shropshire Imperial Yeomanry during the

Top of page: The Qualicum Beach Hotel, 1931. Image from the author's postcard collection.

THE QUALICUM BEACH HOTEL, QUALICUM BEACH, B.C.

Boer War from 1900 to 1902.[5] He returned to England and married Maud Boileau Wood, second daughter of Edward Wood of Culmington Manor, Shropshire.

In 1912, Money journeyed to Ontario and then to British Columbia to enjoy some fishing and see the country. He stayed ten days at Qualicum Beach and liked it so much that he purchased six lots and made plans to build a hotel and golf course. To finance the venture, he created and sold shares in the Merchants Trust and Trading Company, of which he eventually became the managing director. "The Trust registered in BC in 1910 and its shareholders came from Newcastle-on-Tyne in north-eastern England. Its purpose was to invest in mortgages and property."[6] The company opened the new Qualicum Beach Hotel in 1913.[7]

The two-storey Tudor structure reflected the British connection of both the owners and the majority of the European population who lived in the village at the time. As guests arrived at the front entrance of the hotel, they would walk up the six steps of a wide stairway onto a large porch, where other guests could be seen relaxing in large, comfortable chairs and enjoying the view of the golf course and the beach in the distance.

Facing page: The
Qualicum Beach Hotel,
ca. 1955. Image from the
author's collection.

Money returned to England and brought his family back to live in Qualicum Beach in February 1914. But the Qualicum Beach Hotel had barely got off the ground when the Great War broke out that summer. Money was forced to put his plans on hold and do his duty by returning to England to rejoin the British army. Given the command of the Royal West Kent Regiment with the rank of colonel, he sailed to Alexandria, Egypt, in March 1916 to take up his new assignment. While in the Middle East, his command captured the Mount of Olives as part of General Edmund Allenby's liberation of Jerusalem, and in October 1917 Money was promoted to brigadier general in command of the 159th Brigade, Welsh Division.[8] He continued to make a name for himself and was awarded the CMG and bar added to his Distinguished Service Medal. General Money's medals are on display at the Qualicum Beach Museum.

Back in Qualicum Beach, the hotel was converted into a convalescent hospital in 1917. Run by Dr. Campbell Davidson, it housed wounded and convalescing officers for the next three years, and an east wing was added to the building during this time.

General Money returned to Qualicum Beach in July 1919, and in March 1920, the hospital closed, and the property resumed operation as a resort hotel owned by Money and managed by Felix Masarati.[9] The general loved fishing, and he built a cabin dubbed "the money pool" on Stamp River solely for that purpose. The cabin next door had at one time been owned by renowned business tycoon and real-estate mogul John Jacob Astor.[10]

The 1923 summer season was very lucrative for all the resorts in Qualicum Beach. Along with the throng of vacationers who arrived by boat, train, and automobile came a number of distinguished guests to the Qualicum Beach Hotel and golf club, including the King of Siam, writers Edgar Rice Burroughs and Zane Grey, comedian Bob Hope, actors Errol Flynn and Spencer Tracy, actress Shirley Temple, and the list goes on. Obviously,

Brigadier-General Noel Money's campaign medals on display at the
Qualicum Beach Museum. Photograph by the author.

the secret was out that the east coast of Vancouver Island was a desired vacation getaway spot for both stars and regular folks,[11] and the charming hotels and cabins in the resort towns of Parksville and Qualicum Beach were fully booked during the busy summer season.

F. Zimmerman was the assistant manager to the manager General Money at the hotel through the 1920s. In 1926, a group of First World War veterans gathered for a meeting in the laundry room of the Qualicum Beach Hotel and decided to form a branch of the Royal Canadian Legion for the village of Qualicum Beach.[12] Money was elected as president of the Qualicum Board of Trade a few years later, in November 1929, shortly after the stock market crash. He held this post until November 1936.[13]

The ripples from the Great Depression soon made their way to Vancouver Island, and Money found that he could not pay his groundskeeper, Frank Topliffe, for the full season that they were opened—March to September—so Money had to reduce Topliffe's employment to April through to September throughout the 1930s.[14] To make ends meet, Money was forced to sell sections of the eighteen-hole golf course for development as residential lots.[15]

In October 1939, Maud Boileau Money, the general's wife, died from cancer. She was seventy-two years old, and in addition to her husband, she was survived by their son, Gordon, of Vancouver and daughter, Mrs. Mary E. Denny, of Qualicum Beach. General Money was now alone and in failing health. Son Gordon was busy with his duties in the Canadian Army and was, therefore, not available to help with the operation of the hotel, so Money decided to form the Qualicum Beach Hotel Company and sell his beloved hotel in 1940. The following summer, Money died at the age of seventy-four at his home at Qualicum Beach.[16]

The Qualicum Beach Hotel Company continued to sell off small parcels of land throughout the 1940s. Control of the company passed to Fraser McIntosh and Alistair Cummings, who hired Mrs. F. George Walker as manager. In 1954, Arthur Brown, manager of the Vancouver Club (Mrs. Brown managed the Ladies Club of Vancouver), purchased the Qualicum Beach Hotel for the sum of $105,000. The Browns ran the hotel as the Qualicum Beach Inn until they closed the business in 1969.[17] The old hostelry sat empty until 1972, when it and the remainder of the hotel properties (except the golf course) was sold to a developer, who built thirty houses that he put on the market for sale.

BOWSER HOTEL
1925—1969

The E&N Railway finally completed tracks from Parksville to Courtenay in 1914. Bowser was a stop along that line at mile 22, north from Parksville. The community received its name in 1915 from the seventeenth premier of British Columbia, William J. Bowser.[18] A mix of logging, farming, and fishing sustained the local economy until vacationers discovered the area when the E&N came along and added important tourism revenue. Today, the area from Qualicum Bay to Union Bay, including the village of Bowser, is known as Lighthouse Country.

The scenic view of the Strait of Georgia was spectacular as the E&N Railway hugged the shoreline at a number of points along the way from Qualicum Beach to Qualicum Bay then into Bowser. The journey took passengers over a series of short bridges crossing Kinkade Creek, Qualicum River, Nile Creek, and finally Thames Creek just as the train entered the station at Bowser to take on and drop off passengers and to exchange mail bags.

Ridership increased in the warm months from April to September as vacationers sought out the many resorts and hotels in the area, including the Bowser Hotel, located just across the street from the train station and general store. It was one of the more modest hostelries along the E&N route, but it managed to amass a remarkable history in its forty-four

Facing page: Bowser Hotel, owners feeding wildlife, ca. 1940. City of Vancouver Archives 586-386.

years of existence, including a fascinating tale about a former employee in the beer parlour who became rather famous.

Built by Joe Charlebois in 1925, the modest rancher-style Bowser Hotel was situated at the bend in the Island Highway between Qualicum Beach and Union Bay. Charlebois later added a gas station and a dance hall beside the general store and post office across the unpaved highway from the hotel. It was a good time to build in Bowser. Local logging companies, the local mill, and the small but lucrative fishing industry were all on hiring sprees, and the community was growing with the influx of workers and their families.[19]

While the hotel was under construction, Charlebois applied for a beer parlour licence, which had just become available that year. When the licence came through, the first in line for a beer was Jack Holt, Bowser's postmaster until 1955.[20] A veteran of both the Boer War and the First World War, Holt also ran the general store and post office in Bowser. He could rarely be found there, however. Holt loved his beer, and once the Bowser Hotel beer parlour opened, locals who had business in the post office knew where they could find the postmaster.

Holt became a regular customer in the beverage room, where he would spin yarns about his time in South Africa to anyone who would listen. Some evenings he would become so inebriated that he had trouble making his way across the dirt highway that separated the hotel bar from his store. Sometimes he wouldn't quite make it home, and instead was found passed out and sleeping in the middle of the road just yards from his front door. After a while, a waiter or one of his drinking buddies would put the drunken postmaster into a wheelbarrow and take him home.[21]

In 1928, Charlebois sold the hotel to Cecil "Cappy" Winfield and his wife, Florence, who soon had more than Jack Holt to contend with. With Cecil as proprietor and his brother Charles as bartender, the new owners experienced a rough start when Charles was fined $300 under the Liquor Act for selling beer to underage customers in the beer parlour. That was a vast sum of money back in 1928, but the punishment reflected the seriousness of selling beer to minors. In this case, it contributed to the deaths of two young men who crashed their automobile at the foot of Sandhill in Deep Bay.[22]

The Winfields put their hotel and the village of Bowser on the map by their choice of particularly unusual employees. The hotel and beer parlour was a menagerie (not including some of the customers) in which Cecil and Florence trained a deer, a racoon, a bear cub, and two dogs in the fine art of customer service—it was like an episode of *The Waltons*, cute and homey. The most famous of them all was Mike, a black and white English sheepdog–terrier cross that learned how to carry a bottle of beer in his mouth and bring it to a customer's table. Mike even collected payment in his teeth and deposited it in the correct slot in the cash register. He then ran back with any change owing as well as a bottle opener. Mike the bartending dog was so good at his job that he earned a place on the hotel sign. "At closing time and when the last customer had left, Mike would slam the door with a resounding bang. 'Go and Shut the door Mike' was Cappy's command."[23]

Mike's escapades drew international attention as New York papers caught hold of the story, and *Life* magazine featured an article about the smart pooch and his offspring, Ritzi.[24] Mike was also considered for a silver medal by the New York Anti-Vivisection Society for intelligence and loyalty.[25] He was often sent across the road to the store to fetch chocolate bars or snacks, and even Jack Holt got into the act and sent Mike on errands to bring back mail so the postmaster didn't actually have to leave his beer. Mike was also a big hit at birthday parties and was honoured with his own party on his seventh birthday. Kids came from miles around to meet and celebrate with Mike on his special day.[26] The owners were all smiles as word spread about Mike. They enjoyed the notoriety, but even more, they loved the additional business.

One day in 1941, Mike was sent on a routine errand to the store but never came back. When Cappy went to look for the dog, he found him at the side of the highway, severely injured. Mike had been hit by an automobile, and the driver had left the scene. Heartbroken, the Winfields were told that Mike would not survive his injuries. After Mike died, he was buried at the back of the hotel. A slab of granite was used as a headstone, and written on it was one simple word: MIKE. The owners trained Mike's offspring, Ritzi, to perform the same duties, but she didn't possess the same ability as old Mike (or make as much in tips).

The Winfields sold the Bowser Hotel in 1945, at the end of the Second World War. The hotel continued in business for another twenty-four years, going through changes and different proprietors along the way. In the hotel's final days, Jack Holt, quite elderly by that point and disconcerted that his legacy could be upstaged by a dog, continued to warm his seat at his favourite table in the Bowser Hotel beer parlour. When asked how he'd like to go to his maker, Holt replied that he wanted to pass away in the beer parlour with a beer in his hand. He almost got his wish; he died from heart failure as he was entering the pub just steps away from his favourite table.

In the early hours of a Saturday in May 1969, the Bowser Hotel went up in flames and could not be saved. For years after the fire, the lot sat empty save for some burned remnants from the hotel fire and a solid piece of granite that marked Mike's grave. After a few more years, it, too, was gone, swallowed up over time by the wild brambles while drivers rushed past on the widened paved highway, unaware of the events that once took place there all those years ago.

NELSON HOTEL
1893–1955

The six miles from Bowser to Fanny Bay revealed lovely coastal scenery as the E&N route passed Deep Bay, then hugged the sea-shore through Mud Bay leading up to a short run into the small

oceanside community of Fanny Bay on Baynes Sound. The name Fanny Bay first appeared in the 1864 edition of the *Vancouver Island Pilot* based on surveys by Captain G.H. Richards of the Royal Navy, but exactly who Fanny was remains a mystery. It may have been named for the wife of Admiral Hornby.[27] By the time the railroad arrived in 1914, the economy was driven by logging and mixed farming. Oyster seeding was introduced in 1913, 1925, and again in 1942. But it wasn't until 1947 that major clam and oyster seeding became economically viable.[28] In 1938, the year that the Fanny Bay Hotel was built, the population of the tiny community fluctuated between 168 to 250 people, depending on the success of the local logging camps.

Postcard depicting the large and elaborate Nelson Hotel when Union Bay was a mid-sized town. From the author's collection.

Opened in 1893, the Nelson Hotel was built during an economic boom in Union Bay. An attractive hamlet hugging the central east coast of Vancouver Island, Union Bay was blessed with a deep-sea harbour, and since the late 1880s, it had been transformed into an important shipping port for coal.

In 1888, Robert Dunsmuir had purchased the Union Wharf (built the previous year by the Union Coal Company) and expanded

Above: The Nelson Hotel Bar ca. 1915. Image 990.24.311 courtesy of Courtenay and District Museum.

Below: Postcard of the Nelson Hotel ca. 1949, a few years before it was destroyed by fire. From the author's collection.

Coke Ovens, Union Bay, B. C.

Coke ovens and wharf at Union Bay, 1904. Image from the author's collection.

its facilities to process and store the large quantities of high-grade coal produced at his mine in Cumberland, in the Comox Valley, before it was loaded onto ships for export to worldwide markets. Dunsmuir hired approximately two hundred Chinese labourers from Wellington mines to clear land and lay tracks from the Cumberland colliers to Union Bay, and by 1889, Union Wharf was fully operational.[29]

To house the influx of workers and shipping crews and provide the amenities they needed, Union Bay grew into "something of an instant town,"[30] eventually peaking at a population of ten thousand people.[31] George Howe, an entrepreneurial butcher in Cumberland, saw an opportunity to cash in on the busy port, so he purchased land in Union Bay and arranged to have it cleared for the development of the first hotel in town.

Born in England in about 1849, Howe had immigrated to Canada in 1876 and was one of the first pioneers to settle on Hornby Island in the Strait of Georgia.[32] He opened his first butcher shop at

Comox in 1882 (though he kept his Hornby Island ranch to serve as his future retirement home), then moved his business to 2637 Dunsmuir Avenue in Cumberland in March 1890 after buying out the local butcher, Mr. Gladden. While living upstairs from his butcher shop, Howe installed a bath with hot and cold running water, the first in town.[33]

Living in Cumberland, Howe witnessed first-hand the growth in Dunsmuir's coal mine, and he realized the opportunity to add other businesses beside his lucrative butcher shop. In addition to the land and hotel investment he made in Union Bay, he bought a boarding house in Cumberland.

By August 1893, with his magnificent thirty-room Nelson Hotel nearing completion, Howe sold his butcher shop in Cumberland to Francis A. Anley and moved to Union Bay.[34] In addition to serving as a hotelier, Howe opened a general store—using the billiards room as a temporary space until a larger building was erected next door—and served as the community's first postmaster, also from his store (the magnificent post office building that survives to this day replaced the post office in Howe's store in 1913).

In addition to all of the coal-shipping activity in town, Union Bay became a regular stop for CPR steamships, whose passengers filled the rooms at either the Nelson Hotel or the Wilson Hotel, built in 1898. Hotel guests also included the crew and captains of the up to fourteen deep-sea vessels that arrived at the port each month and waited their turn in the harbour to take on coal. One such man, Captain Fletcher of the steamer *San Mateo* out of San Francisco, came ashore to the Nelson Hotel bar one day and made a deal with George Howe to circumvent customs and smuggle tobacco into Canada. Unfortunately, their conversation was overheard, and when word got out to the local customs agent, George Rowe, he had the pair arrested. They were convicted of smuggling and fined $500 each.[35]

Howe ran the popular Nelson Hotel until he sold out to John A. Fraser and Charles R. Bishop in August 1907. He returned to his ranch on Hornby Island, where he accepted a job as supervisor of roads. In February 1915, Howe was appointed provincial election commissioner for Hornby Island, and he lived and worked there until his death in June 1916 at the age of sixty-seven. He is buried at the Sandwick churchyard two miles northeast of Courtenay.[36]

The partnership of Fraser and Bishop lasted from 1907 to 1933, through the golden era for the Nelson Hotel, the store, and the town of Union Bay. The Fraser and Bishop store was the largest on the island north of Victoria by 1913.[37] In the spring of that same year, a significant event occurred in the store that certainly deserves mention.

Near midnight on March 3, 1913, provincial police constables Gordon Ross and Harry Westaway saw a light in the Fraser Bishop store and cautiously crept over to investigate. Ross slowly turned the knob to the front door and slipped into the store, with Westaway following close behind. Quick as a flash, a shot rang out from a .44 revolver just as Ross made out two figures hunched behind the store counter.

The two were Henry Wagner, dubbed "the Flying Dutchman," and his accomplice Bill Julian, who had been on a robbing spree of businesses in the waterfront communities of central east Vancouver Island. Wagner once rode with the notorious Hole-in-the-Wall Gang out of Wyoming, which had included Butch Cassidy and the Sundance Kid, and he had so far escaped capture by us marshals in the American southwest to British Columbia. Wagner and Julian lived in a shack on Lasqueti Island in the Gulf of Georgia, which they also used as a hideout to plan their robberies.

Using the twin-engine power boat *Spray*, which Wagner had stolen in Puget Sound, the two bandits had been entering coastal communities under the cover of darkness and robbing uninhabited cabins and closed retail stores, looking for anything of value. Until Wagner and Julian came along, most store owners didn't feel the need to lock the doors at closing time. Wagner and Julian's modus operandi was to arrive by boat late at night, load it up with stolen loot, and make a speedy escape. What they didn't account for was the prospect of dealing with provincial police who were expecting them to show up in Union Bay. Apparently, Wagner and Julian had preyed on Union Bay on two previous occasions, and Chief Constable David T. Stephenson had suspected their return. Rookie constables Ross and Westaway were assigned to support the regular constable of the area, Jack McKenzie (nicknamed "Big Mac"), for just such an eventuality, and now here they were, being shot at in the Fraser Bishop store.[38]

The bullet grazed past Constable Ross's arm and lodged square in Constable Westaway's chest. Julian lit out as fast as he could, but Wagner stood his ground, his handgun pointed right at Ross. The rookie policeman immediately lunged for the gun, and a struggle ensued. Ross endured repeated blows to the head from a desperate Wagner until the constable was finally able to get a hand free, grab his nightstick, and subdue Wagner with a number of blows to the stomach and head. The last hard crack to Wagner's head made him groan and slump to the floor.

Both men were bloody and beaten by the time Constable McKenzie, who had heard a shot and then glass breaking, arrived to assist Ross. As he cuffed Wagner, McKenzie called out for assistance, and soon a doctor arrived to patch up the wounds of the combatants. Unfortunately, it was too late for Constable Westaway, who died from the bullet wound in his chest.

Wagner was thrown in jail and charged with murder. Meanwhile, a frightened Julian had stolen a rowboat and made the long journey back to his cabin hideout at Lasqueti Island, only to be apprehended by constables sent to stake out the place.[39]

Julian "was in deadly fear of Wagner" and gave evidence of other crimes that the two had committed. He received a lighter sentence for his testimony as a Crown witness.[40] The defiant defendant Wagner was found guilty of second-degree murder and sentenced to hang.[41] The execution was set for Nanaimo on August 25, 1913, which just happened to be Constable Ross's birthday. As the last day of Wagner's life approached, the thief and murderer became less defiant and twice attempted suicide to cheat the hangman. His first attempt took place in his jail cell, where he ran as quickly as he could into the iron bars in hopes of breaking his neck. He only ended up injuring himself, and a doctor was summoned to patch him up. Wagner then tried to strangle himself with his bedsheets but was thwarted by an alert jailer. He remained under watch until the following day, when he was escorted to the gallows and the sentence was carried out.[42]

Once Wagner was dispatched by the law, things calmed down at Union Bay and across the central east coast of Vancouver Island— but not for long. In February 1922, a fire in Union Bay consumed half the town before it could be brought under control. The commotion started at about three in the morning, when the night watchman spied some smoke pouring out of Dale and Broder's General Store, next door to the Wilson Hotel. Soon the hotel itself was on fire, and it was reduced to ashes within fifteen minutes, according to eye witnesses. The size and ferocity of the fire must have been terrifying for onlookers, especially when the hot water tank inside the Wilson Hotel exploded with such force that the sheet iron was almost flattened.[43]

Fortunately, there were no fatalities, and only a few people sustained minor injuries, but property damages amounted to well over $30,000. In addition to the general store and the hotel, the fire destroyed Smart's Butcher Shop, Hudson's Residence, the medical offices, and a few garages and other outbuildings.

There were a couple of lighter moments during and after the fire. Mr. Boyce, who lived above the medical building, had gone outside to see what the fuss was all about in the earlier stages of the fire. He was wearing only his night cap and pyjamas, and as he walked outside, the door had closed shut behind him; he had to wait for firefighters to knock his door down so he could get to his clothes. Also, one poor American sailor staying at the doomed Wilson Hotel had just paid his rent in advance when his room and board burned from under him and he lost everything he owned. Some would say that's just bad luck, but this was the second time this fellow had been "burned"—he had suffered a similar fate in a hotel in Portland, Oregon, when he paid rent in advance only to witness the place destroyed by fire. "He now swears by all the stars in Old Glory that he will never pay in advance again," reported the *Cumberland Islander*.[44]

The Nelson Hotel was one of the few survivors of the fire, as the Wilson Hotel, its closest competition, was destroyed. Fraser and Horne ran their general store and hotel from 1918 to 1932, expanding in that period to add ten more rooms, for a total of forty. In March 1925, the hotel was granted a beer parlour licence, not only making the loggers happy to be able to drink in a bar again, but also making the owners happy to once again have the revenue from the sale of beer after such a long dry spell.

On May 22, 1955, the wonderful old Nelson Hotel met the same fate as the Wilson Hotel, and many a hotel before and since, when it was totally destroyed by fire. Ironically, the fire department had purchased a new fancy fire truck that year, but it was not delivered in time to save the hotel.

By this time, Union Bay was a shadow of its former boomtown self. Demand for coal had started to wane in the early 1920s, replaced by other fuels such as oil. The fortunes of the village were directly tied to the coal facilities, and as business fell off, the town experienced significant downsizing. Union Wharf closed down for good in the early 1960s.

The Riverside Hotel,
Courtenay, B. C.

CUMBERLAND
MILE 218

COMOX
MILE 234

CHAPTER 8

Cumberland to Comox

THE VILLAGE OF CUMBERLAND WAS built on coal. From 1852, when coal was discovered in the area, until the mid-1960s, the black gold was the mainstay of the economy.

The pioneer days of Cumberland, or Union as it was initially called, began when the Union Coal Company was set up in 1869 to mine coal on a claim called Coal Creek in the Comox Valley, southwest of present-day Cumberland.[1] In 1883, Robert Dunsmuir and Sons bought out the Union Coal Company and other smaller coal-mining outfits in Comox. In February 1888, Dunsmuir sent a prospecting party to explore if it was feasible to mine coal and determine the best location to start a mine. They chose Coal Creek, later called China Creek, to open their Union mines, and the settlement that grew out of the mining activity was called Union.[2] Dunsmuir and his son James "transformed a tiny coal camp into an important coal-producing community."[3] James Dunsmuir later renamed the growing town Cumberland in honour of those coal miners who arrived from Cumberland in Great Britain.[4]

From 1888 through the 1890s, Cumberland saw a frenzy of building and land clearing in the sea of tree stumps. Muddy in the wet months and dry and dusty in the summer, the town grew as more businesses opened up. Among these new businesses were hotels such as the Union Hotel, the Victory, the Vendome, the

Cumberland, the King George, and the Waverley, built to house the influx of miners and other labourers.

Postcard showing the train station at Cumberland. From the author's collection.

These hotels provided a clean place to sleep, hot meals, and most importantly, a bar. Mining work is thirsty work, and each of the non-temperance hotels had a full bar, especially on Saturday nights. Our next stop is at one of the new hotels, the Waverley Hotel, built in the booming 1890s.

WAVERLEY HOTEL

SINCE 1894

The Waverley Hotel (also spelled as "Waverly" over the years) was the second hotel built in the burgeoning town of Cumberland, opening in July 1894 as a three-storey temperance hotel managed by Alexander Lindsay. Hotel rates were set at six dollars per week or twenty-five dollars per month; single meals cost fifty cents, or one could buy a twenty-one-meal ticket for five dollars.[5]

When the lease was transferred to John Usworth in 1896, a bar was added and he was granted a liquor licence, and the premises were enlarged considerably with the addition of two buildings to the north of the original. The inclusion of a bar should have

generated a tidy profit for the hotel, but Usworth left the owners and staff high and dry by running off with the money meant for paying employees.[6]

That setback aside, the Waverley Hotel bar—affectionately referred to as the "Hug and Slug"—became a favourite haunt for thirsty miners. Saturday night was especially busy, for that was the night that patrons could shake off the coal dust accumulated through the week by drinking and dancing the night away.

After Usworth flew the coop, a number of managers came and went, including John Richardson and Frank Crawford (1897–1902), Samuel and Mary Shore (1902–1907), and Richard and Ann Coe (1907–1909). The Coes had immigrated to the United States from England and become American citizens before moving to Vancouver Island in 1899 and making their home in Cumberland, where their two sons worked in the Dunsmuir mines. Initially they managed the Union Hotel on Dunsmuir Avenue until leasing the Waverley Hotel in 1907. Upon leaving the Waverley in 1909,

Richard became the night watchman for the town, affectionately known to all as "Dad" Coe.[7]

In October 1909, Frank and Domenica Dallos took over as the new owners of the Waverley Hotel. One of their first initiatives was to clear the lot next to the hotel and erect an additional building, which today houses the private liquor store for the current owners of the Waverley Hotel.

The Dalloses were both born in Torino, Italy—Frank in 1865 and Domenica (née Chioda) in 1881. At the age of eight, Frank worked as a "water boy" at the Suez Canal. He immigrated to New York City at age eleven and worked his way across the United States. By 1889, he was working as a coal miner in the Extension–Nanaimo mines on Vancouver Island, and by 1898, he had opened a wholesale liquor store in Cumberland with partner John Tha.[8] (Frank sold the liquor business to Mr. Mussatto before buying the Waverley

Plaque located on the outside of the Waverley Hotel. From the author's collection, 2008.

Hotel.)[9] Domenica immigrated to Canada in 1894 and married Frank in Nanaimo.[10]

A few years after the Dalloses purchased the Waverley Hotel, they rented it to the provincial police for use as headquarters during the Big Strike of 1912–1914, when the police were brought in to control striking coal miners.[11] The rent that they received allowed them to invest money in a sawmill at Royston. On June 28, 1918, their daughter, Kate, completed her nurse's training at St. Joseph's Hospital in Victoria. Her proud parents attended the graduation ceremony, after which Frank took his daughter's hand and led her outside onto the street, where he presented her with a brand-new Chevrolet automobile.[12]

The Dallos family continued to operate the Waverley Hotel through the difficult times brought on by Prohibition. They must have continued doing something right because they built an addition to the hotel in 1920. However, in January 1922, a fire in downtown Cumberland destroyed three stores, one being Campbell's Meat Market, owned by Frank Dallos. The loss was estimated at $6,000, and Frank had no insurance.[13]

By 1925, Prohibition was over in the hotel industry. Frank's application for a beer parlour licence was granted on March 31 of that year, making the Waverley Hotel among the first in town with a licence, along with the Cumberland and the Union. It must have been a sight to see when the doors of the beer parlours opened for the first time since Prohibition had closed the saloons and hotel bars seven years and six months earlier. That's a long time to build up a thirst! The government-controlled beer parlours were nothing like their freewheeling counterparts of the past—singing, dancing, eating, standing while drinking your beer, mixing with the opposite sex, and playing cards or games such as darts or billiards were all banned in the beer parlour, as was buying cigarettes (you had to bring your own).[14] Basically all you could do was sit and drink copious amounts of cheap draft beer, but that was all right with the majority of customers. They were just happy that the bar was back.

The ability to sell beer again proved very lucrative not only for the Waverley, but for most hotels in British Columbia. However, many soon learned that the new rules handed down from the BC government were very strict. Within days of being granted a beer parlour licence, Dallos and two other beer parlour operators in Cumberland were charged with violating the Liquor Act and fined $300 each, with the alternative of three months in jail.[15] Exactly what these proprietors did to deserve such a harsh sentence is unknown, but I suspect that they jumped the gun and sold alcohol before their licences arrived.

In December 1925, the Dalloses were involved in a serious automobile accident. While returning from a funeral in Nanaimo, their car skidded over some gravel left on the highway from a road scraper, causing it to flip right over. Frank was driving, and there were six other passengers, including Domenica and their daughter, Mrs. W. Gordon, in the vehicle at the time. Frank and his daughter suffered only minor injuries in the accident, but Domenica's leg was crushed. The other passengers also sustained minor injuries, the most serious being Mrs. Balagno, whose leg was badly fractured when it was pinned under the car after it finally came to a stop.[16]

The family had to endure another hardship when young Grant Dallos, Frank and Domenica's four-year-old grandson, underwent an operation for appendicitis in 1927. Fortunately, the boy survived.[17]

On January 30, 1929, the local newspaper reported that Frank was seriously ill. The sixty-four-year-old patriarch of the family was admitted to Cumberland Hospital. Money had been generously spent to modernize the facility with the most up-to-date equipment, so Dallos was in good hands, and he soon regained his strength and returned home to convalesce. But in late March, Domenica found him slumped over and unresponsive in his easy chair. He was immediately taken again to the hospital, where he languished in a coma until he died. The hotel and beer parlour were willed to Domenica, but she found it too difficult to run the business. She sold the Waverley to George Spencer in September 1929 and retired to a house on First Street in Cumberland built by her son Fred. She lived there until she died in 1953.[18]

Unlike most of the structures in Cumberland, the Waverley Hotel survived the great fire of 1933, but fire did eventually affect the old hotel when it destroyed the top floor of the three-storey building in the 1960s. In addition to removing the damaged top floor, owners Claude and Hazel Jordan moved the front entrance and stuccoed the exterior. Other renovations through the years to the interior of the historic building made it look a little different than it did when Frank and Domenica Dallos owned it, but the Waverley Pub, nicknamed "the Wave," still serves up friendly home-style food and beverages, making it a favourite for travellers and locals alike. I should know, because I bought the T-shirt.[19]

RIVERSIDE HOTEL

1890 – 1968

After Robert Dunsmuir established a major mining interest in Union, which later became known as Cumberland, in 1888, the influx of workers and businesses also helped develop the town of Courtenay—named after George William Courtenay, captain of the British ship HMS *Constance* stationed in the area between 1846 and 1849. Courtenay was located on the opposite side of the Puget River from Cumberland, and a bridge already joined the two communities—though the E&N Railway didn't arrive in Courtenay until 1911.

One of the more striking-looking hotels built before the arrival of the E&N, the Riverside Hotel opened in 1890. Initially it was a modest and genteel two-storey wood structure with a long porch at the main entrance and rooms on the top floor with a front-facing balcony. The entire hotel was subsequently raised—affording it an extra storey— after which the bar was re-established on the ground floor.

This attractive ornate building was constructed by owner John J. (Johnny) Grant at what is today the corner of Fifth Street (changed from its original name, Union Street, in the 1940s) and

Cliff Avenue. Like many other buildings erected in Courtenay and Union (Cumberland), the Riverside was built with lumber from the Grant-Mounce Sawmill, which Johnny's brother Robert leased from Dunsmuir.

Before entering the hotel business, Johnny Grant won the contract to build the Colonization road that ran eight miles from the Comox harbour to Black Creek, which greatly helped settle those areas over the years.[20] The Riverside Hotel had daily stagecoach service on the Colonization road and into the wilds beyond. The stage was connected to the steamships and to the E&N Railway when it finally arrived in Courtenay in 1914.

The Riverside Hotel attracted guests from all walks of life, but especially catered to hunters, fishers, and loggers. Grant advertised regularly to let it be known that "large game abounds in the Courtenay area and that trout were plentiful in the Courtenay River."[21]

Postcard of the Riverside Hotel after expansion ca. 1919. From the author's collection.

Grant also promoted the hotel bar, stating that Billy Glennon, his head bartender, had "a reputation of being the best bartender in the province."[22] An idle boast or true, it didn't really matter, as the Riverside Hotel bar didn't really require much advertising. Business was brisk, especially on Saturday nights when loggers filled the bar and drank all evening until closing. "Stories abound of liquor flowing freely, high-stakes gambling in the back rooms, men riding a stuffed elk and the police not far away, ready to intervene when the inevitable fight broke out."[23] "It was a place for loggers to stay and socialize—it never cut a swath like the Comox Hotels did."[24]

Grant married Jenny Grieve of Sandwick, a small farming community located on the Tsolum River in the Comox Valley. Although the Grants retained their ownership of the Riverside Hotel, they leased it out to a succession of proprietors; W. Sharp, George Dunbar, Mr. Mulligan, and William E. Glennon each took their turns running the hotel from 1895 to 1900. During this period, the Riverside Hotel hosted various social events, of which the weekly dances proved very popular.[25] And like at most hotels raffles were held for prizes like the "new domestic Singer sewing machine" awarded to the winning one-dollar ticket.

In the summer of 1896, the Riverside Hotel and other businesses were threatened with destruction when a fire broke out in a nearby residence. A last-minute shift in the wind saved the hotel from the flames.[26] As we shall see, this was not the only time that the Riverside Hotel would be in such peril.

In September 1898, owner Johnny Grant fell gravely ill. As the weeks went by, Grant's health deteriorated to the point where his brother Robert took him to the capable hands of Doctor Jones at the Jubilee Hospital in Victoria. The doctor did all he could, but Johnny Grant died at the age of forty-two on December 13, 1898. Robert brought his brother's remains back from Victoria to be buried at the Presbyterian Church cemetery at Sandwick.[27] Johnny's former bartender, Billy Glennon, was one of the pallbearers at the funeral, and Glennon went on to lease the Riverside Hotel for a number of years before becoming its new owner in 1900.

Glennon spruced the hotel up with a new coat of paint inside and out. He continued the popular dances and raffles in the hotel and added other social activities, such as shooting matches: "Don't forget the Grand shooting match at the Riverside Hotel in Courtenay, Xmas Day; Plenty of Birds. Shooting begins 11 a.m. Bring your guns,"[28] read one announcement in 1900—because there is nothing quite like celebrating Christ's birth by shooting fowl. Hunting and fishing were two of the most popular pastimes on Vancouver Island one hundred–plus years ago, when game was plentiful. On occasion, the hotel would put unusual items on display, such as the "monster turnip" that weighed in at just over sixty pounds. The circumference of this unusually large and heavy root vegetable was four feet two inches at its widest.[29]

In the autumn of 1907, Otto Fechner purchased the Riverside Hotel from the Reifel brothers of Nanaimo. During Fechner's tenure, the hotel went through a major modernization and expansion, doubling in size to a total of twenty-nine guest rooms. For the reasonable rate of $2.50 per day, guests were offered rooms that were as "clean as a new pin, well ventilated, and very comfortable, and a cuisine that would suit an epicure."[30] Fechner also bought a handsome new eight-seat autobus for picking up and dropping off guests at the E&N station (when it finally arrived in Courtenay) and at the CPR docks in Comox. In all, Fechner ended up spending $18,000 on the Riverside Hotel expansion and update.[31] It was money well spent, as the 1913 summer tourist season was the best on record. Courtenay was growing at a very rapid pace, and the local hotels were so busy that they often had to turn customers away.[32] The coming of the E&N in 1914 fuelled expectations that this local boom would continue—and indeed it did. On January 1, 1915, the city of Courtenay was officially incorporated.

Meanwhile, the popular dances continued at the Riverside. In August 1915, Mr. and Mrs. Fechner celebrated their silver wedding anniversary with an extravagant banquet and dance at the hotel. Music was provided by the Cumberland Band, who performed from the balcony above the spacious dance floor. The dance was attended by members of the elite and most of the business community, but Fechner did not forget the workers—especially the loggers who filled his hotel bar every Saturday night.

Fechner was a good businessman who appreciated his loyal customers. The Riverside Hotel bar was the favourite watering hole of the loggers, and Fechner knew that they came to play hard and spend money. "For a time he acted as an unofficial banker to the loggers, who received no pay from the company until their contract was over. It was a safe venture for Fechner: he would advance the cash, and the company would repay him directly at the end of the contract. This practice ended when the company began to pay the men regularly."[33] It helped that the hotel was located next to Comox Logging's main rail line; sure-footed loggers could jump from one of the sixty passing train cars and run into the hotel bar for a quick beer before dashing back out in time to catch the last train car.

In the summer of 1916, the Riverside Hotel was again threatened with destruction from a fierce fire that consumed the nearby Opera House and wiped out most of the businesses on that side of the street. By one-thirty in the morning, the forces battling the blaze had to dynamite a number of houses in order to stop the flames from destroying the hotel.[34] The Riverside was saved once again— but unlike a cat, the hotel did not have nine lives. On a cold January morning in 1968, the Riverside Hotel burned to the ground.

Mr. and Mrs. W. Mueller were the proprietors at the time, and the hotel bar (beer parlour) was still a popular place for loggers and other travellers seeking to quench their thirst. Up to thirty firefighters fought the blaze while the hotel's night clerk, Harry Fenton, ran through the hotel during the early stages of the fire, knocking on every hotel door to alert guests to the danger. His efforts paid off. Out of the twenty-eight guests and staff in the hotel at the time, only three people were taken to hospital with smoke inhalation, and no one was killed.[35] The lovely historic Riverside Hotel was not so fortunate, however. "Nobody understood how important the hotel was to the community until it was gone ... it was Courtenay's landmark for seventy-nine years."[36]

LORNE HOTEL

1878—2011

Although the E&N did not have a direct line into the community of Comox, its close proximity to Courtenay as the northern terminus and the three historic hotels there—the Elk, Lorne, and Port Augusta hotels—make Comox an important part of the history of Vancouver Island hotels.

The oldest of the three main communities in the Comox Valley, the village of Comox (originally called Port Augusta after one of Queen Victoria's daughters) was first proposed in 1861 by Sir James Douglas, who saw the potential for farming in the valley and encouraged settlement. The Royal Navy played an important role in the early development of Comox, transporting settlers, implements, and produce to the community. "Although some unofficial settlers had arrived in previous years, the first government-approved settlers arrived in 1862 aboard HMS *Grappler*. Scottish immigrant James Robb, age 44, and his son William realized that the shoreline along the former K'ómoks fishing village and the Great Comox Midden was sheltered from the prevailing southeast winds by the sandy hook of the Goose Spit and would be the only place between the Courtenay River and the Spit suitable for landing supplies."[37]

In 1874, Joseph Rodello used government money to build a wharf at Port Augusta, just a mile east of Robb's land. Once the wharf was in operation, the fortnightly visit by steamer was an essential lifeline for the small community, and the beginnings of a town took shape as businesses and houses were built. The Port Augusta Hotel opened near the wharf, and its main competitor, the Elk Hotel, was located directly at the foot of the wharf. The third historic hotel

built in Comox, the Lorne, was just up the street, and that's where we shall visit next.

The Lorne Hotel in Comox ca. 1890. Image 977.9.4 courtesy of Courtenay and District Museum.

The Lorne Hotel was built in 1878 on the corner of Wharf and View Streets by Californian carpenter John Fitzpatrick, and it was most likely named after the Marquis of Lorne, who married Princess Louise, one of Queen Victoria's daughters, and was Governor General of Canada from 1878 to 1883. The original structure was built with hand-hewn beams cut from trees that still had the bark showing.[38]

Fitzpatrick, who had gained experience running a hotel and bar when he briefly leased the Elk Hotel from owner Joe Rodello,[39] "fitted up the Comox Hotel [Lorne] with a special view to the comfort and convenience of invalids, tourists and sportsmen."[40] The hotel was also popular with sailors off the navy ships that paid frequent visits to Comox (naval officers tended to stay at the competing Elk Hotel, especially when the McDonalds ran it—not because it was any better than the Lorne, but because the McDonalds had several beautiful and talented daughters of marrying age). Over time, the modest two-storey Lorne Hotel also became a community gathering place for picnics, games, dances, traditional holidays, elections, wakes, and special anniversaries like the Queen's birthday and Dominion Day—it was simply the place to go to get the most up-to-date local and international news.

In December 1883, Fitzpatrick leased the Lorne Hotel to Samuel and Florence Cliffe for the sum of $2,000.[41] Samuel (Sam) Jackson Cliffe was born on June 10, 1840, in Brewood, Staffordshire, England. He was twenty-two when he left Liverpool with his brother Robert on the steamship *Silistria* on July 11, 1862, for the long voyage to Victoria. Little did Cliffe know that his future wife, six-year-old Florence Harmston, was aboard the same ship with her parents, Mary and William from Lincolnshire, who had planned to start a new life in either New Zealand or Australia but changed their minds when they read a notice about available land in the Comox Valley.[42] The decision to settle at Comox and disembark from the *Silistria* most likely saved their lives, because after the ship left Comox, it picked up a load of lumber in Port Alberni and continued west, "only to disappear without a trace in a tropical storm."[43] Meanwhile, Sam and Robert Cliffe, who had disembarked at Victoria in November 1862, got caught up in the frenzy of the Cariboo gold rush. After a brief and unsuccessful attempt to strike it rich in the Cariboo, the brothers returned to Victoria, then made their way up island where they dabbled in prospecting around the Cumberland area.[44]

In April 1872, Sam Cliffe married Florence Harmston at St. Andrews Anglican Church, the first marriage to take place in Comox.[45] The couple took up farming, and over time Florence gave birth to fifteen children, of which ten survived into adulthood. In 1883, they leased the Lorne Hotel.

In those days, the consumption of alcohol was a generally accepted part of life for many pioneers. "Adults drank at home, at work and at play, usually every day and often all day."[46] Not everyone imbibed, but those who did at the Lorne Hotel received a bonus with their five-cent beer or ten-cent cocktail from the great teller of tails himself, Sam Cliffe. "Sam was a big bearded man who always told funny stories. Florence managed their family of ten children and acted as barmaid and cook."[47] Cliffe could keep customers entertained (and drinking) with yarns that became more nonsensical as the night wore on. Reports like the following were common in those early days: "At Comox, nearly all the settlement turned out to a grand dance in the Lorne Hotel on Thursday evening and a 'right royal' time was had dancing from dewy eve till early morn. Mr. Cliff [sic] makes a genial host."[48] The consumption of liquor, and especially whisky, was so pervasive that it began causing problems in the small community, and for a while the Lorne Hotel's liquor licence was revoked, though it was reinstated two years later.[49]

Pleasant (and generally sober) events also took place in the Lorne Hotel in those early years. One such occasion saw the Cliffes' daughter, Florence, marry Arthur Radford of Courtenay. The smell of orange blossoms filled the air as the couple exchanged vows at the United Church of England west of Courtenay. The ceremony was followed by a delicious dinner and dance hosted by the proud parents at the Lorne Hotel. "Music arose with a voluptuous swell and all went as merry as a wedding bell. It was a gathering long to be remembered."[50]

The Lorne Hotel was threatened with destruction in the summer of 1906, when a fire broke out in the district and started to grow out of control. Thanks to "a heroic fight by a volunteer [fire] brigade," the Lorne Hotel and surrounding businesses were saved.[51] Fire has always been the biggest threat to the hotels, and as we shall see, dodging this threat in 1906 only delayed the inevitable end of the Lorne.

Two years after the threat from the Comox fire had passed, Sam Cliffe, "the jovial, good natured story-teller,"[52] pioneer, father of ten, and friend to all, died in July 1908 at the age of sixty-eight.[53] Florence

Proprietors of the Lorne Hotel, Emily,
Cap, and son Ken Fairbairn ca. 1940s.
Photograph courtesy of Barb Tribe.

continued running the Lorne Hotel until March 1912, when she sold it to George M. Barlow. Florence died in 1929. After Prohibition came into effect in October 1917, the loss of bar revenue forced the Lorne Hotel to close, and it wasn't opened again until new owners bought the empty hotel in 1921 and gave it a new lease on life. The new owners were the Fairbairn family, and they successfully operated the Lorne Hotel for the following thirty-eight years, until 1959.

Maurice G. Fairbairn, whose nickname was "Cap," managed the Riverside Hotel in Courtenay for eight years before setting his sights on the forlorn Lorne Hotel in Comox. Fairbairn and his wife, Emily, saved the historic hotel from an uncertain future by renovating and updating it. In March 1925, they applied for and were granted a beer parlour licence after completing the necessary modifications to satisfy the new liquor control regulations. The beer parlour was divided in two; one area was for men only while the other area was reserved for women and their escorts (though Cap never approved of ladies drinking).[54] The rooms were quite basic, with wooden tables and chairs in a spartan atmosphere, and as stipulated by the liquor control board, there was no food service and no games were permitted. The only thing one could do was to sit and drink beer. Evidently, the Fairbairns did not put all their hopes in the beer parlour; they also played host to forty guests during an afternoon tea in order to raise funds for the local community hall.[55]

When Cap died in 1946, Emily became the sole proprietor. With the assistance of in-laws Peggy Fairbairn and Ken, Emily ran the hotel with good common sense and did the bulk of the work, right down to cleaning the laundry.[56] Emily's two granddaughters occasionally visited, staying in the hotel's attic above the kitchen. In the morning, they went downstairs to the bar before opening time to help clean up, and they were allowed to keep any coins found on the floor. Emily managed the hotel until 1953, when she sold it to the Grant family, who eventually sold it to George Taylor.[57]

The last owner of the Lorne, when it was called the Lorne Pub, was George Kacavenda, who operated it for fifteen years until a fateful day in February 2011, when the 133-year-old structure was destroyed by fire. Starting in the centre of the historic building at around one-forty-five AM on February 28, the blaze soon engulfed the entire structure. The thirty firefighters combating the fire didn't have a hope of saving the iconic pub, so they concentrated their efforts on protecting nearby businesses.[58]

Nothing quite compares to the sense of loss to a community when it is suddenly deprived of one of its historic buildings. A connection with the past is severed; it's like losing an old friend. In the days after the fire, former customers and employees fondly recalled time spent at the Lorne Pub; perhaps it was a splendid luncheon, or an evening drinking up a storm with friends, or an intimate moment with a loved one. "Bert and I met in the Lorne Hotel on July 10, 1981 and we have been together ever since," said one patron. "I cried when it burned down."[59]

Above: The Lorne Hotel. By the time this photo was taken, the hotel no longer offered rooms but became a landmark in Comox offering great pub food. Photograph by the author, July 2008.

Below: A rare view of the bar in the Lorne Pub. Photo by the author, July 2008.

Left: The Lorne Pub sign. Photo by the author, July 2008.

Below: Aftermath of the Lorne Pub fire, February 2011. Photograph courtesy of Brian Smith.

CAMPBELL RIVER
MILE 280

FORBES LANDING
MILE 294

CHAPTER 9

Campbell River to Forbes Landing

THE CANADIAN PACIFIC RAILWAY, WHICH purchased the
E&N in 1905, originally intended to extend the line northward from
Courtenay to Campbell River and as far as Duncan Bay. "Iron has
been discovered in the Comox District . . . the new discovery will
hasten the building of the railroad from Campbell River north,"
reported one newspaper in 1911.[1] A route was surveyed, and prep-
arations were made to put shovels in the ground, but those plans
were shelved in 1914 with the outbreak of the First World War, and
they were never revived.

As a result, Courtenay remained the end of the line for the
E&N Railway, and people who wished to travel north from there
had to go by road or steamer. But although the E&N never reached
Campbell River and beyond, I have included in this chapter the
two major historic hotels of Campbell River, the Willows and the
Quinsam, as well as the Forbes Landing Hotel, located seven and a
half miles west of Campbell River at Lower Campbell Lake.

Once passengers disembarked from the train at Courtenay,
they had the option to take a stage to Campbell River. The Comox
Valley was a pleasant and green place in the spring and summer
months, and the thirty-one-mile journey from Courtenay was relatively easy; it was also very scenic, with rolling hills, farms, and
stretches of forest.

The Hudson's Bay Company traded with the Komenox (Comox) peoples, part of the Lekwiltok First Nations, as early as the 1820s. The paddle wheeler *Beaver* was used during trade trips to Indigenous villages along the coast in 1836.[2] But European settlement in the area was still many years off.

In September 1879, the steamship *Princess Louise* brought C.E. Hunter and his party to the mouth of the Campbell River to pursue the exploration of Comox District,[3] and in 1883, a logging camp was built, and a few scattered farms were established. Through the 1880s and 1890s, an increasing number of homesteaders moved into the area just south of the mouth of the Campbell River. These early European inhabitants were occupied in farming, fishing, mining, and logging. By 1901, the region from Oyster Bay to Rock Bay contained a number of logging camps, which were organized into the District of Sayward.[4]

But it was the arrival of the Thulin family, and in particular the opening of their Willows Hotel in 1904, that finally sparked the town of Campbell River to grow.[5] The new hotel not only provided a comfortable place for sports hunters and fishers to stay, but also promoted the benefits of living and working in this land of opportunity and great abundance.

WILLOWS HOTEL
1904–1963

For a time, the Willows Hotel *was* Campbell River. The city we know today grew out from the hotel, which was a fixture on the landscape for almost sixty years. There were actually three Willows Hotels through the years—two were destroyed by fire, and one was repurposed for another use. The first Willows Hotel was built by Charles and Fred Thulin and opened on July 1, 1904.

Charles August Thulin, later nicknamed "Poppa Thulin," emigrated from Sweden in 1887 at the age of twenty-four. After working his way across the American Midwest, he arrived in

Above: First Willows Hotel and annex, 1904. Photo by Henry Twidle, Helen Mitchell Collection. Image 8248 courtesy of the Museum at Campbell River.

Below: Second Willows Hotel, 1908. Photo from the Carl Thulin Collection. Image 10257 courtesy of the Museum at Campbell River.

Above: The third and final version of the Willows Hotel in 1931. Image from the author's collection.

Below: Williams at Willows Hotel bar, 1914. Photo from the Helen Mitchell Collection. Image 7143 courtesy of the Museum at Campbell River.

Vancouver just as that city was recovering from the great fire two years earlier. Thulin worked in Port Moody for a short time before trying his hand at logging at Lund on the Sunshine Coast. Thulin and his wife, Maria (Mary) (née Johanson), who was also from Sweden and whom Charles had met in Vancouver, raised their three daughters, Anna, Elin, and Lillie, and son, Carl, in Lund.

In 1889, Thulin's brother Fred joined him in Lund, and the two became business partners, first opening a small store, then adding two hotels, a mine, and a towboat in that community.[6] As Lund grew, the Thulin brothers prospered. By 1904, they owned and operated the Malaspina Hotel in addition to their general store and post office. But Charles was always on the lookout for the next business opportunity, and he found it west of Lund across the Strait of Georgia in a small community called Willow Point on Vancouver Island.

The area around Willow Point was still made up only of a handful of settlers and a series of logging camps. It was a beautiful area and quite suitable for building a hotel and the Thulins' second home. The Thulin brothers, with partner Emerson Hanna, visited the area around Willow Point and soon found a location to build the original Willows Hotel, a two-storey, thirteen-room facility that took about three months to finish.[7] Many feel that the hotel's official opening on July 1, 1904, marks the beginning of the city of Campbell River. It was certainly the beginning of the Thulins' reign as the long-term owners of one of the best-known and most popular hotels north of Victoria on Vancouver Island.

Soon after opening, the Thulins added a "loggers annex" about five hundred yards north of the main hotel, offering loggers their own rooms at sixty cents a night. From there it was a short walk to the hotel bar, a popular place for loggers during their time off. These men of the woods worked hard and played hard, and this was especially true on Saturday nights when the Willow bar would fill to capacity with thirsty loggers looking to get drunk and to blow off a little steam. Whisky and beer were the most popular drinks; a shot of whisky cost ten cents and a mug of beer a mere five cents. The cacophony emanating from the busy bar grew increasingly louder as the night wore on and the alcohol flowed. To stem the tide of complaints from guests about the noise from the bar, the Thulins decided to move it into the annex. Even so, the sounds of revelry drifted through the air to the nearby main hotel, resulting in complaints the following morning from cranky guests who had got little or no sleep.

"Charles Thulin was a dynamo, the driving force behind an impressive inventory of enterprises . . . he was a good-natured man, known by all as Poppa Thulin."[8] In 1908, Charles and Mary Thulin and their family permanently moved from Lund to Campbell River. They also decided to build a new and larger Willows Hotel a bit closer to the all-important Campbell River wharf, where CPR steamships brought passengers and goods into the core of a developing downtown. The original hotel was converted into a loggers' annex, and the original annex was renovated into the cleverly named Uneeda Laundry.

On July 1, 1909, approximately five hundred people gathered to celebrate the grand opening of the new Willows Hotel. The future certainly looked bright for the Thulins and for the town of Campbell River, but it was not to last. Less than eight months after its gala opening, the second Willows Hotel burned to the ground. Mr. Thompson, the hotel's bookkeeper, was killed in the blaze.

Plans were immediately drawn up for a third Willows Hotel to be built on the site of the second. On July 1, 1910, this final version of the hotel, more magnificent than the previous two, opened for business. "A Victoria visitor, H. Johnson, marvelled over the sophistication and elegance of the third Willows Hotel, he added in his journal: 'Loggers are restricted to one end of the hotel, and the corridors leading to their rooms are separated from the rest of the hotel by partitions and closed doors, so that the loggers, if inclined to be boisterous, will not interfere with patrons of the hotel of quieter instincts.'"[9]

September 29, 1917 was the last Saturday before Prohibition came into effect in British Columbia. It was also the last chance for the hard-working, thirsty loggers of the area to enjoy one final big party before saying goodbye to John Barleycorn. With approximately three hundred loggers expected to fill the bar until closing, it promised to be quite a night. Thulin added extra staff, but he stood by in case some kind of brouhaha erupted—a likely event any time you get hundreds of drunken loggers together in a room. "Within two hours the hotel's beautiful tiled floor was awash with broken bottles, glasses, window panes and broken furniture . . . the fun developed into a full-scale brawl . . . until son Carl Thulin quickly boarded over the broken doors and windows to bar the men's return."[10]

After Prohibition became law, Thulin kept the bar open and sold a product labelled "near beer" that contained only the small percentage of alcohol acceptable under the new rules set by the government. Customers hated it, and as the dry months stretched into years, the bar sold ice cream and soda pop to sports fishermen and tourists. Thulin also partially made up for the loss of liquor revenue by opening the Lilelana Pavilion near the main hotel, named after their three daughters, Lillie, Elin, and Anna. The pavilion was a place for dancing and music recitals and proved popular from the end of the Great War into the 1920s.[11] When the bar finally reopened as a beer parlour in March 1925, it looked very different from the original.

The Thulins promoted their hotel as a haven for sports fishermen, spending a substantial amount of money on advertising that big Tyee salmon were plentiful in the waters off Campbell River and that the same could be said for freshwater trout in the rivers and lakes in and around town. An Indigenous person caught nine adult Tyee salmon in less than a day during an exceptional fishing season, and it was true stories like that that kept the sports fishermen coming, filling the hotel to capacity. Guests who missed out on a room had the option to camp on the hotel grounds.[12] Thulin hired Melville Haig to manage the hotel and to promote local sports fishing. Haig eventually started the Tyee Club of Campbell River, which held meetings inside the Willows Hotel and advertised in BC *Outdoors Sports Fishing* magazine. Campbell River became world-renowned as a mecca for fishing Tyee salmon, and the Willows coined itself the headquarters of the salmon capital of the world. It was no idle boast.

In 1927, the Thulins felt it was time to retire, and they sold their precious Willows Hotel—all three versions of which had proved to be a great success for the family and the community—to Gertrude and Stanley Isaac. Five years later, in April 1932, "Poppa" Thulin passed away. "Hundreds of people from all over the coast flocked to town to pay their last respects to the old pioneer."[13]

The Isaacs ran the hotel from 1927 to 1944, with Gertrude managing the hotel portion, and Stanley running the bar (and continually working his drinking arm). The couple bought a parrot that became a fixture (not literally) in the Willows Hotel lobby for the amusement of hotel guests.

By 1954 the BC Liquor Control Board allowed for a new type of drinking establishment that would be quite unlike the beer parlour—the cocktail lounge. The only stipulation was that the cocktail lounge had to be a part of an existing or new hotel. Hotels all over BC began applying for cocktail lounge licences, and those that were granted licences quickly began building their lounges. In March 1955, with Joe Iaci in charge, the Willows Hotel, having been granted a cocktail lounge licence, opened the Sou'easter Room located across from the large, popular beer parlour. Cocktail lounges introduced a whole new and sophisticated place where adults of both sexes could drink together, unlike in beer parlours. The lounge at the Willows Hotel was tastefully decorated in greens and brown and included two large murals depicting—what else— sports fishing and hunting on Vancouver Island, painted by artist Paul Soldatkin. All that and a spectacular view overlooking the Strait of Georgia made for a magical evening.

When owner Joe Iaci died in April 1961, his nephew Frank Iaci arrived from Vancouver to look after the funeral arrangements and to manage the Willows Hotel. Frank was still in charge and looking for a new owner to buy the aging hotel when disaster struck. In the early morning hours of January 19, 1963, guest Herman Quocksister had just checked into the hotel and gone up to his designated room when he noticed smoke coming from under the door of room 38. He immediately notified the night clerk at the front desk, and by the time the two went upstairs, the whole hall was filling with smoke. Quick thinking by Quocksister saved a number of lives that morning as he went to every door he could reach, shouting that a fire had broken out. In the meantime, the night clerk appeared to do everything wrong. He did not sound the fire alarm because guests may have mistaken it as a burglar alarm; instead, he opened the door to room 38, which immediately gave the flames inside a rush of oxygen, and what had been a small fire roared into a torrent of flames. The fire doors were not closed, and one fire exit was blocked.

It took the fire less than one hour to devour the old hotel while desperate guests ran and jumped from windows to escape being burned to death. Four people died—David Lowe, Sven Lindgren, Gerald Heenan, and Charles Knutson—and eight others were injured,[14] but the toll could have been much worse if not for the heroic efforts of Herman Quocksister and of ordinary citizens like Douglas Pierce, who while watching the hotel burn learned that a man was still in one of the rooms. Pierce ran to the back of the burning structure and climbed the fire escape, then located the unconscious man and pulled him out of the smoke-filled room and onto the fire escape, saving his life. Four local boys helped Pierce carry the man to safety.[15]

In the tragic blaze, Campbell River lost the Willows Hotel, "one of its most tangible links with its past."[16] It was later decided that the hotel would not be replaced. The property sat vacant for years. In 1986 the Willows Neighbourhood Pub opened in Campbell River by Al Thulin, grandson to Charles and Mary Thulin, and his wife, Sue. The pub ran for twenty-eight years before it closed on March 30, 2014, just shy of 110 years from the day the Thulins opened the first Willows Hotel.

QUINSAM HOTEL

1917 – 2017

The Willows Hotel was about to have competition from another hotel that had a meagre beginning but grew in popularity over the next few years to rival—but not quite equal—the Willows. The Quinsam Hotel, in Campbellton, just north of Campbell River city limits and eventually swallowed up into Greater Campbell River, goes back to 1917, when Mr. T.W. Hansen began building a modest-sized hotel. Hansen did not get far into the construction when he ran into financial difficulties that forced a stoppage in work, and he dubbed the yet unnamed hostelry "the white elephant." He sold the property to Thomas Laffin, who picked up where Hansen left off and completed the building, naming it the Quinsam Hotel, only to be faced with Prohibition in October 1917. Shut off from the potential revenue from the bar, Laffin sold the hotel to Ken Bergstrom.[17]

The colourful Bergstrom, nicknamed "Brannigan," drove a cab for a living; he also ran a neat little bootlegging service on the side. In his younger years, Brannigan had worked as a "powder monkey"—the person responsible for detonating dynamite—but he left that line of work after a stick of dynamite blew five of his fingers off in a horrific accident.

In 1923, Brannigan sold the small hotel to James (Jim) "the Bishop" English. Born on February 3, 1884, in Durham, England, English had moved to Vancouver Island when he was a young man and had eventually landed in Oyster River, where he ran a store and the Fisherman's Lodge. He also liked to dabble in bootlegging, and apparently made a tidy profit off this activity. English purchased

Quinsam Hotel in 1925, May Baldwin Fonds. Image 7686 courtesy of the Museum at Campbell River.

the Quinsam Hotel from monies he had earned in his successful oyster business.[18]

English immediately began making improvements to the hotel, replacing the original flat roof with a peaked one and shingling it with the assistance of Carl Thulin, the son of the Willows Hotel owners. English also expanded the two-storey Quinsam Hotel by adding a restaurant and a barber shop on the ground floor. He continued to invest in the Quinsam Hotel, and by 1927, he had enlarged the existing rooms and added several new ones.

As to the many silly stories about why English had the nickname "the Bishop," perhaps none are as beer-soaked or ridiculous as the following. English was said to be serving some friends and customers in the beer parlour when one of his regular patrons appeared to have fallen asleep with a glass of beer on the table.

Jim English and friends in Quinsam beer parlour in 1963 smiling away, from the Archie Waldref Fonds. Image 8023 courtesy of the Museum at Campbell River.

English tried waking the man until he realized the customer was not in fact sleeping, but dead—which probably explained why he had been drinking the same glass of beer for the past few hours. English and a handful of close friends discussed the situation and decided to form a late-night procession to the cemetery, where English presided over the body of the poor stiff and recited the last rites before burial. I'm not sure many believed this story outside of the beer parlour, but it did land Mr. English with the Bishop moniker.[19]

Through his long thirty-five-year tenure at the Quinsam Hotel, English would take on partners that included Micky Pierce, John Rosconi, and Jack Ross, and it was Ross who finally bought the retiring English out in 1959. Ross continued the work of expanding and modernizing the hotel, including doubling the 125-seat pub and creating quite a large beer parlour that tended to fill up on Friday and Saturday nights, mainly with mill workers, loggers, trades people, sports teams, and other blue-collar workers. By the 1950s and 1960s, regulations for beer parlours were relaxing to allow the serving of other drinks besides draft beer; cider, wine, and bottle beer were all available to wash down hot pub grub.

On August 16, 1961, Jim "the Bishop" English died. But the English name continued in connection with the Quinsam through his son, Bob English, a junior partner in the hotel with manager and co-owner Jack Ross. In the summer of 1963, Ross and English spent upward of $100,000 giving the exterior of the Quinsam Hotel a totally new facade and canopy with "banks of attractive florescent lighting under the canopy . . . (that would) glow green through the plastic." Now that's '60s class. They also renovated the interior; "the lobby was completely overhauled with rich wood panels, an angled registration desk and [more] up to date lighting."[20]

In September 1974, Ross sold the hotel to the Katz family, who changed the name from the Quinsam to the Kerdon Hotel. According to Katz, every letter in the new name represented a word: Katz, Eli, Rachel (Eli's wife), Dov (their son, and apparently the "d" also stood for "dumb"), an unknown word for O, and Narcissus (their daughter). Only the immediate Katz family and first-time out-of-town visitors called it the Kerdon, however; to everyone else, it was the Quinsam. In 1976, Korchula Enterprises purchased the hotel and George Alto became the manager, and the first thing the new owners did was change the name back to the old familiar Quinsam.

The Quinsam Hotel supported local teams and sponsored many different sports, such as a bowling team that won second prize in the 1982 season of the Annual Bowling Bonspiel held in Chilliwack. But along with the good times was the dark side of operating a hotel with a large drinking establishment attached. In July 1985, two people were charged with murder after an Alberta man who was staying at the hotel and drinking in the pub was robbed and beaten while outside having a cigarette. He died from head injuries suffered from the beating.

The evening of June 27, 2017, while patrons of the Quinsam Hotel were enjoying themselves in the pub, and a handful of guests were in their rooms preparing for bed, the fire alarm suddenly began ringing forcing everyone out into the parking lot. The Quinsam Hotel had caught fire, and it was later learned that it originated in one of the rooms in the upper part of the hotel. I was researching the history of the Quinsam Hotel when my wife and I found out that fire had destroyed the historic hotel and pub. We had gone to the hotel six months earlier. It was our first visit to the Quinsam, and we were surprised then saddened when we learned of its demise.[21]

Most people have happy memories of the Quinsam Hotel, from enjoying the great live music, to laughing with friends while sharing some good times and good memories through the years. The hotel had been threatened with closure a number of times, but someone always seemed to arrive at the eleventh hour and keep the place alive. Fred from Port Alberni was the last owner to keep the Quinsam from closing, and it looked like the old hotel had some years in her yet. But fire, the bane of many an historic hotel, may have closed the Quinsam forever, relegating the hotel to the history books.

FORBES LANDING HOTEL
1911—1974

We end our journey seven and a half miles west of Campbell River down a road that deposits us at the foot of a pleasant resort overlooking the south shore of pristine Lower Campbell Lake. It's called Forbes Landing, and to get there, one had to board a bus along the Gold River Highway (now Highway 28), then just a narrow dirt road.[22]

The Forbes Landing Hotel was built by James Forbes, a native of Wick, Scotland. Born on January 20, 1883, Forbes immigrated to

North America, first settling in Montana and finding work as a saddler, then moving to Victoria, and finally arriving in Campbell River in 1910.[23] Forbes got a job with the Campbell River Power Company, monitoring the flow of Elk Falls. He also worked in a variety of side jobs, including harvesting poles for Cudahy Timber. While working for Cudahy, Forbes travelled extensively through the area and quickly grew to love the lush green wilderness and abundant rivers and lakes.

A postcard of the Forbes Landing Hotel ca. 1915. Image from the author's collection.

Forbes especially enjoyed one spot that had a remarkable view of the Lower Campbell Lake, where he spent a night taking in its enormous beauty. One can imagine him warming himself by the fire and watching the sun set in a kaleidoscope of colours that gradually dissolved into the gloaming and later drifting off to sleep to the sounds of the crackling fire and an occasional mournful cry from a bird that echoed out from some dark place and travelled on the ripples of the lake, which were further stirred up by trout gathering in flies for their evening meal.

Forbes woke the following morning refreshed by a good night's sleep and knowing that this was the place where he would build

Forbes Landing

his home—and he knew just who he wanted to share it with. Forbes had been dating a local girl, Elizabeth Sutherland, and in 1911 they married.

The newlyweds were a good match; they shared a love of the outdoors and had a mutual goal of making a living at Forbes Landing. Elizabeth had a background in the hotel industry, and Jim worked as a guide, taking visitors by horseback on day trips along the trails. It was during one of those guided tours that Forbes learned from a local surveyor that the first provincial park was planned near Forbes Landing.

The Price Ellison report commissioned by the provincial government recommended that 530,319 acres of pristine wilderness be set aside for the first provincial park on Vancouver Island. It was to be called Strathcona Park.[24] The news that a park would likely open at his doorstep piqued Forbes's interest, as he saw the potential for a lucrative sports fishing and guiding business in addition to a hotel. Forbes bought the property he loved from Cudahy and work began to build the Forbes Landing Hotel. Selective logging by the Cudahy Timber Company in the early 1900s had preserved most of the trees near the shoreline where Forbes chose to build.

The original hotel was a ten-by-twelve-foot houseboat. "Lumber was brought to the southern shores of Lower Campbell Lake by horse and wagon and from there to the building site by canoe which proved to be slow and arduous. While building his floating hotel Forbes worked as a guide for timber cruisers and surveyors involved with the new provincial park."[25]

The floating hotel's first year in business was very successful until a winter storm damaged the structure so severely that it could not be salvaged. Undaunted, the Forbeses agreed to abandon the idea of a floating hotel and instead build a more traditional structure by the lake. Construction began in the autumn of 1913. The main hotel, outbuildings, and a dock were built first, later followed by a number of guest cabins. The Forbeses received help from Elizabeth's brothers, Jasper, Walter, and Bill Sutherland, in exchange for employment as packers and guides during the busy tourist season.

The hotel was completed the following spring, just in time for the opening of the hunting and fishing season. The new hotel offered a warm, clean, comfortable, and modern place for guests. Most rooms had a splendid view of the lake, and complimentary rowboats were available for guests to go fishing or sightseeing.

Most visitors came to Forbes Landing for the fishing. The lake was teeming with rainbow and cutthroat trout in those early years. It was an angler's paradise, and unlike most fish stories, the stories coming out of Forbes Landing did not need embellishment. "The Len Harding party landed eighty fine trout on these lakes while the Redpath party secured large catches of trout on nearby McIvor and Echo Lakes. The guests agree that excellent fishing combined with the pristine natural scenery result in a very pleasant stay at the Forbes Landing resort."[26] Photographs showing proud sports fishermen displaying their catches were commonplace.

The phone directory for 1918 described Lower Campbell Lake as "a fisherman's paradise that drains into nineteen chartered lakes, many of which have never been fished."[27] This was sports fishing on a grand scale, and the abundance seemed endless. It was just a matter of time before fish stocks began to decline and conservation and even restocking the lakes were necessary, but for now, it was a free-for-all with no limits.

The road from Campbell River to Forbes Landing, then on to Strathcona Park, was greatly improved in 1916, allowing easier access. The comfortable resort in the wilderness was close to the improved road, and this plus an aggressive advertising campaign made the 1917 season the most successful yet as an influx of curious campers and sports enthusiasts poured into the area. Having by now completed the guest cabins, the Forbeses and Sutherlands were ready for the new arrivals. Jim Forbes invested in an express engine for the twenty-eight-foot teak-hulled boat that he used to ferry guests across Lower Campbell Lake to the prime fishing spots.

The spectacular setting, ease of access, and gentle conviviality of the hosts made Forbes Landing a desired destination, and the word got out. It wasn't long before newspapers as far away as New York and Los Angeles published stories about the excellent fishing that could be had in the beautiful surroundings of Forbes Landing on Vancouver Island.

Living and working at Forbes Landing must have been exciting during those early years. In addition to the large quantity of fish, there was plenty of game to be had, including deer, bears, and cougars. In the winter of 1922, Jim Forbes's beloved hunting dog, Buster, had a confrontation with a hungry cougar. The two got into a fight that ended when Buster chased the animal back into the bush. Buster lost a paw in the fracas and had to spend months recuperating at a Vancouver veterinary hospital before returning to her master in a joyful homecoming.[28] Cougars were a menace to local ranchers, farmers, and residents alike, so the provincial government offered a forty-dollar bounty for the capture or carcass of the large cats.

With all the hunting that went on, there were bound to be accidents, some minor and others serious or even fatal, like the one that occurred in November 1922. An Esquimalt man, Fletcher B. Cousins, was hunting deer with a few buddies when, in his haste to catch up to a deer, his rifle got tangled in the bush, and a shot rang out, hitting him and killing him instantly. In another incident, three Boyd brothers from Cumberland were deer hunting when they lost track of the time and it grew dark. With no proper supplies or even matches to start a fire, the brothers were ill prepared for a night in the woods. Fortunately, this story has a happy ending, as they were found the following day, cold and damp after a long night in the wilderness.

The most destructive event to take place at Forbes Landing became known as the Great Sayward Fire of '38 or the Great Bloedel Fire. Whatever it was called, it destroyed everything in its path, including the Forbes Landing Hotel. The summer of 1938 was abnormally hot and dry; a prolonged heat wave began in the spring and continued into July with no sign of rain. Fears of a fire increased as the long hot dry spell continued.

And sure enough, on July 4, sparks from a passing train caused a small fire to break out in a pile of slag timber at camp 5 of the Bloedel, Stewart & Welch Logging Company, just north of Campbell River. The fire was promptly discovered, and the actions of the employees brought it under control. It looked as though the fire was extinguished, but overnight winds stirred up the hot embers from the initial fire and sparked spot fires that quickly grew in size. The Bloedel employees were rapidly overwhelmed by the ferocity of these new fires, fanned by ninety-mile-per-hour winds.

As the fire escalated over the following weeks, everything in its path came under threat, including the Forbes Landing Hotel. By day thirteen of the fire, the Forbeses and their forty guests were told to evacuate. Despite the order, a few guests insisted on staying to watch the approaching flames, but they were quickly convinced to leave for Campbell River as the wall of flames destroyed the guest cabins, dock, boats, outbuildings, and the Forbes Landing Hotel itself.

In the end, the fire raged on for almost six weeks and destroyed 74,495 acres of timber before it was finally under control.[29] Campbell River survived thanks to a change in wind direction away from the city. After the fire was finally put out, rumours of sabotage began, including that fire hoses had been cut and that sugar had been added to the water pumps to render them useless. "Incendiaries were responsible for the spread of the fire by unemployed men from Vancouver who needed the work," read one newspaper report.[30] It was believed that Forbes Landing could have been saved if it weren't for these acts, but although the accusations were investigated, nobody was ever charged with any offences.

Jim and Elizabeth Forbes lost everything, but fortunately they had insurance and would build again. The Forbeses were not bitter, and they thanked everyone who had worked hard to try and save their resort. "They've done all they could, the forestry boys, the loggers, provincial police and game wardens," said Jim. "They put up a great fight to save this place."[31]

The Forbeses loved their lodge in the wilderness, and the feeling was shared by the hunting and fishing sports community. The third version of the Forbes Landing Hotel opened on June 1, 1939, on the very same spot as the previous hotel. Three hundred guests were invited to join the Forbeses in their celebration of the gala event. "They came from all over Vancouver Island and Vancouver to gaze on the new thirteen-room Forbes Landing Hotel."[32] It was bigger than the previous lodge, and it now offered the most up-to-date conveniences with the same down-home comfort and service that guests had come to expect from its congenial hosts. The dock, cabins, and outbuildings destroyed in the fire were also rebuilt.

As the 1939 season came to a close in November, the lakes in the area began to rise from days of heavy rain. The Forbeses got their feet wet in the basement of their lodge from the minor flooding that occurred, but there was little damage. Perhaps this was a warning of what was to come when the whole of Forbes Landing would be underwater.

MOVING FORBES LANDING HOTEL FOR FLOODING OF LOWER CAMPBELL LAKE.

Postcard showing the moving of the hotel to higher ground before the completion of the
Campbell River dam, June 1949. Image from the author's collection.

When the Second World War broke out in the autumn of 1939, it was business as usual at Forbes Landing. The hotel enjoyed an international reputation as an excellent wilderness getaway, an escape for those who wanted to rest, enjoy the great outdoors, and forget about the troubles of the world, if only for a little while. The Forbeses continuously advertised their wilderness retreat, and Vancouver Island Coach Lines sold three-day holiday tours to Qualicum Beach, Forbidden Plateau, and Forbes Landing, describing the last as "a 200 mile drive along the island highway to the famous resort of Forbes Landing—meals and lodging included for a total of $18.25.[33] Indeed, many international guests took advantage of the chance to spend some time at Forbes Landing, including Mr. and Mrs. Harpo Marx, of Marx Brothers fame, who stayed at the famous lodge for a week of fishing.[34]

The Forbeses had survived a great fire and a minor flood, but Mother Nature wasn't finished yet. On the morning of Sunday, June 23, 1946, a strong earthquake measuring 7.2 on the Richter scale shook the region, toppling chimneys at the epicentre of Campbell River and creating chasms over a wide area. The quake lasted for thirty seconds but remained in the memories of the residents for a lifetime. There was one fatality.

The next challenge the Forbeses had to face didn't come from nature but from a major man-made hydro-electric project that directly threatened Forbes Landing and their livelihood. Post-war plans for the growing region forecast an increased demand for electricity, and a series of dams were proposed for the Campbell River, to be built in stages from 1947 to 1951. When completed, these dams would supply Campbell River and the region with enough hydro-electric power for the foreseeable future, but they would also raise the water level on Lower Campbell and connecting lakes as high as fifty feet which would totally immerse Forbes Landing and turn the three existing pristine lakes into one massive body of water.[35]

Once the massive dam project received the go-ahead from the government, the Forbeses had no choice but to strip the hotel clean and move it before it was swallowed up. After thirty-five years in business, it looked as though they were finally beaten. Friends and neighbours rallied to the aid of the Forbeses and the lodge they all considered a home away from home. A number of schemes were floated to save the hotel. One idea was to construct a log float around the hotel, which would allow it to float as the lake level rose. A more practical idea was to dismantle the hotel and rebuild it on a new site near the edge of the rising lake. The Forbeses' resignation turned to hope as they accepted an offer to raise the structure, place it on skids, and tow it out of harm's way with two giant diesel tractors. Son Gordon Forbes moved the hotel with the assistance of a crew so skilfully that not a cup was broken, and the family remained in residence during the ten days it took to complete the project.[36]

Once the Forbes Landing Hotel was secure in its new location, business resumed as before to the relief of its owners and regular guests. Jim Forbes continued working at the hotel until he was sidelined by illness. He died at the Campbell River Hospital on October 10, 1954, surrounded by friends and family. Forbes was seventy-one years old. His widow, Elizabeth, continued to operate the hotel with help from the family until she sold it to Bernard "Kelly" Save in 1962 and retired. Elizabeth Forbes died in Richmond, BC, on April 8, 1987, just shy of her 101st birthday.

After its founders were gone, the Forbes Landing Hotel continued to attract guests, but it was never quite the same. Bernard and Leona Save did add their own unique touch to the thirteen-room lodge, introducing weekend singalongs at the Cougar Room bar. Leona's favourite was "Bill Bailey."[37] One could also play darts or shuffleboard while looking out the windows to enjoy the awesome vistas.[38]

In 1972, the Saves sold the resort to Jack Slade of Haney, BC. Slade's ownership was short-lived. On September 2, 1974,the famous Forbes Landing Resort was destroyed by fire, and it was not rebuilt. Today, Forbes Landing is a privately owned RV park, but the surrounding wilderness is just as appealing as it was when Jim Forbes spent his first night camping by the lake all those years ago.

AFTERWORD

The End of the Line

MOST OF THE MAGNIFICENT HOTELS featured here are long gone, and the few that remain are under threat. Fire, the bane of all-wood-construction buildings old or new, is a constant menace, as we have seen. Time is also a great leveller; it works away at everything, even all of us. The financial situation of individual owners also plays a role in the closing of historic hotels, and increasing land prices sometimes make the option of selling quite attractive. The growth of communities also occasionally forces owners to adapt by repurposing their business. Owners of historic hotels today continue to face all such pressures, and one by one these old hotels are closing.

As for the historic E&N Railway that tied the hotels together, what does the future hold for it? The nostalgic journey we have taken is perhaps more poignant when one considers that E&N Railway passenger service ended in 2011 and may never be resurrected. When the last passenger disembarked from the last passenger train, the controversial conversation began as to whether the E&N was finished for good. At the time of this writing, it does indeed look like the end of the line has come for the E&N. Even the idea of bringing back portions of the passenger service in the Greater Victoria area, with a goal to alleviate the Colwood Crawl, seems to have been rejected by the current BC government in favour of more buses or other solutions.

The E&N's future may not yet be determined with certainty, but we are quite sure about its colourful past and the impact it had on the economies of all the communities it reached on Vancouver Island. Who knows what the communities north of Courtenay would look like today if the E&N's northern terminus had ended at Port Hardy or Cape Scott instead? If that were the case, just think of the additional hotels that would have opened along the way.

In 1963, my father, who worked as a civil engineer for the Royal Canadian Navy, was given an assignment in Victoria on Vancouver Island. Although I was born in Victoria in 1954, we didn't live there long before we were on the move again—such was the life of a navy brat. When I learned that we were returning to Vancouver Island, I asked my dad how big the island was and if I could walk around it in a day. While researching *Along the E&N*, I realized how much I didn't know about Vancouver Island and felt nearly as unaware as I did in 1963. Just as I found out that one cannot walk around the island in one day, I also found that Vancouver Island is rich in history and diversity and that one cannot learn all there is to know about its people and their unique communities in one day or a thousand days. I hope now that you have read this book that you have come away with a renewed sense of the vibrant history of this wonderful island and that you enjoyed your journey into the past along the E&N.

An elderly gentleman watching the demolition of the Tzouhalem Hotel while sitting on an old chair from the pub. Painting of a photograph published in the *Cowichan Valley News*, September 1990, courtesy of Gordon Friesen.

ACKNOWLEDGEMENTS

The increasing multitude of online resources is making research easier than ever. I am thankful to the organizations and people involved in making the following online resources available: the collection of selected BC newspapers from the University of British Columbia; *British Colonist* editions for 1858 to 1970 from the University of Victoria, the *Times-Colonist* newspaper, and other sponsors; the collection of BC city directories for 1850 to 1955 from the Vancouver Public Library; the ever-increasing treasure trove of information and images provided by the Royal British Columbia Museum and Archives; and the recent addition of resources from the City of Victoria. As well, I am so grateful to the community archives up and down Vancouver Island, from Esquimalt to Campbell River, that have been so very helpful and provided many of the excellent archival pictures and images for this book.

Although I did not visit every Vancouver Island community archive this time around, I did manage to get some research time in at Campbell River, Qualicum Beach, Cumberland, Nanaimo, Duncan, and Port Alberni museums and archives. In addition, I have had contact with the Cobble Hill Historical Society's Brenda Krug and Neil Bonner; Lori Treloar and the folks at the Shawnigan Lake Museum; Sherri Robinson of the Esquimalt Archives; and Christine Meutzner, manager of the Nanaimo Archives and connected to the archives in Ladysmith. I urge you to support your local museums and archives who are entrusted with holding and preserving our precious historic artifacts and documents.

I also wish to extend my thanks to the good folks at the Port Alberni branch of the Vancouver Island Regional Library for tolerating all those requests for books. I'd like to think I kept a few people employed just from the sheer volume of requests for materials for this book.

A heartfelt thank you to all those who have contacted me through social media or emailed me regarding family members who were involved in the hotels profiled in this book, from owners and proprietors to bottle washers.

I thank publisher Taryn Boyd, Tori Elliott, Lana Okerlund, and all the other good folks at TouchWood Editions for believing in me and in this project.

Lastly, I thank you, the reader, for purchasing, borrowing out of the library, or stealing a copy. I hope you enjoyed the journey.

Vancouver Island Timeline

1843	Fort Victoria is founded.
1849	Vancouver Island becomes a Crown Colony of Great Britain and is leased to the Hudson's Bay Company.
1849	Fort Rupert is established near the northwest tip of Vancouver Island by the Hudson's Bay Company.
1852	The Hudson's Bay Company begins coal mining operations in Nanaimo, moving their settlement from Fort Rupert.
1853, March 27	Governor James Douglas introduces liquor licences to moderate the retail and wholesale of liquor on Vancouver Island.
1855	The Parson's Bridge Hotel opens (later known as the Six Mile House).
1856	The Parson's Bridge Hotel is granted a country liquor licence after the owner pays a small fine for operating without one.
1858	The region called New Caledonia becomes the Crown Colony of British Columbia.
1858, April 25	The first ships arrive in Victoria with gold seekers bound for the Fraser River gold rush.

1859, May 30	Vancouver Island becomes a Crown Colony as the HBC lease expires.
1860	The Blands open the Halfway House tavern and hotel in Esquimalt (later known as the Esquimalt Inn).
1860	The first export sawmill is opened in Alberni.
1862	An outbreak of smallpox devastates the Indigenous population.
1862, April 14	The steamer *Hermann* arrives in Esquimalt from San Francisco with twenty-three Bactrian camels destined for the interior as pack animals.
1862, August 2	The City of Victoria is incorporated, with Thomas Harris as the first mayor.
1864	Traces of gold are found at Leech River north of Victoria.
1865	Esquimalt is officially declared the main base for the Royal Navy Pacific Fleet.
1864, July 12	The Four Mile House in what is now View Royal is licensed.
1866	Vancouver Island and the mainland are united into a single Crown Colony named British Columbia with the capital at New Westminster.
1868	The capital of the Colony of British Columbia is moved from New Westminster to Victoria.
1870	James Mady and a partner named Peterson open the Goldstream House.
1871, July 20	British Columbia joins confederation with Canada.
1874, December 26	The City of Nanaimo is incorporated.
1877	Sir James Douglas dies.
1878	Richard Watkins opens the Royal Hotel in Nanaimo on the same site where the What Cheer House was located until destroyed by fire.

1879	Andrew J. Bechtel opens the Colwood Hotel.
1880, July 30	The Goldstream Hotel, a larger version of a previous hotel on the same site, opens.
1881	The first census puts the population of Vancouver Island at approximately 17,290 people.
1883, September 27	Robert Dunsmuir incorporates the Esquimalt & Nanaimo (E&N) Railway.
1884, May 7	The first survey for the E&N, Division 1, begins in Esquimalt near Plumper Bay, opposite Inskip Island on the Songhees Reserve.
1884, May 16	The Division 2 survey of the E&N begins from Nanaimo south.
1885, March 5	Construction of the E&N Railway by Division 1 (south to north) begins.
1886, August 13	Prime Minister Sir John A. Macdonald drives in the last spike signifying the completion of the first phase of the E&N Railway at Cliffside near Shawnigan Lake.
1886, November 20	The Morton House at Shawnigan Lake, a stop on the E&N Railway, has its gala opening.
1887, February 7	Samuel and Elizabeth Fiddick open the Occidental Hotel in Nanaimo.
1887, March 24	James Phair opens his elaborate Goldstream Hotel beside the Goldstream House, which is dismantled.
1887, May 3	One hundred and fifty men die in two underground explosions at the No. 1 Esplanade coal mine in Nanaimo.
1887	William Beaumont opens the Alderlea Hotel in Duncan.
1887	Frank H. Price and Percy F. Jaynes open the Quamichan Hotel in Duncan.

1888, March 29	The E&N is extended south from Russell's Station in Esquimalt across the new rail swing bridge into Victoria.
1889, December 15	Three hotels in Victoria are now lit up by electric lighting.
1890	Parksville is officially named after its first postmaster, Nelson Parks.
1891	Samuel G. Lewis opens the Lewisville Hotel near Chemainus.
1892	James A. Porter opens the Station Hotel in Cobble Hill.
1892, April	Matthew Howe opens the Horseshoe Bay Hotel south of Chemainus.
1893, March	Mathew A. Ward opens the Arlington Hotel in Alberni.
1893, July	George Howe opens the Nelson Hotel in Union Bay.
1894	Andrew McMurtrie opens the Abbotsford Hotel in Wellington.
1894, September 28	The Royal Hotel in Nanaimo is destroyed by fire, killing two people and leaving three others (one a little girl) in critical condition from severe burns.
1895	The Hirst family opens the Rod & Gun Hotel in Parksville on the site of their previous hotel, the Seaview, that was destroyed by fire.
1895, December 12	The Colwood Hotel is destroyed by fire.
1896	Tommy Armour and a partner named Chalmer open the Armour Hotel in Port Alberni.
1896, May	The second Colwood Hotel is built over the ashes of the first.
1898	The old Parson's Bridge Hotel is dismantled as the new Six Mile House is built in its place.
1898, September 29	A national referendum is held on prohibition, but no action is taken.

1900	Andrew McMurtrie moves his Abbotsford Hotel in pieces from Wellington to Ladysmith on the E&N Railway.
1900, May 15	On the eve of opening, the Strathcona Hotel at Shawnigan Lake is destroyed by fire. The rebuilt hotel opens on September 19.
1901	The Tzouhalem Hotel, named after Coast Salish Chief Tzouhalem, opens in Duncan.
1901, December 16	The Koenig Hotel (originally the Morton House) at Shawnigan Lake is destroyed by fire.
1902	The new owner of the Armour Hotel in Port Alberni renames it the Somass Hotel.
1902, June 7	The Shawnigan Lake Hotel opens, replacing the Koenig Hotel destroyed by fire.
1904, July 1	Brothers Charles and Fred Thulin open the Willows Hotel in Campbell River.
1905	James Dunsmuir, Robert Dunsmuir's son, sells the E&N Railway to the Canadian Pacific Railway but retains mineral rights.
1908	Mr. N. Brownjohn opens the Buena Vista Hotel at Cowichan Bay.
1909	An explosion at Extension mines kills thirty-two miners.
1911	Strathcona Provincial Park becomes Vancouver Island's first provincial park and wilderness preserve.
1912	Joe Drinkwater and Clive Paxton open the Ark Resort on Great Central Lake near Alberni.
1913	The ss *Oscar* carrying 1,800 kegs of dynamite catches fire and explodes in Nanaimo Harbour; many are injured by flying glass, but nobody is killed.

1914, July	The E&N Railway is completed to Courtenay, with plans to extend the line through Campbell River to Duncan Bay (these plans never come to fruition, however).
1914, July 28	War on Germany is declared throughout the British Empire, including the Dominion of Canada.
1914, August 6	The E&N train takes its inaugural run from Victoria to Courtenay.
1916, August 22	The Shawnigan Lake Hotel is destroyed by fire.
1917, October 1	Prohibition of retail and wholesale alcohol becomes law, leading to a massive closure of hotels on Vancouver Island and across the province as their revenue dries up.
1918, November 11	The First World War ends.
1920, October 20	Prohibition in British Columbia ends in favour of government control of liquor sales and distribution; in a province-wide plebiscite, 92,095 vote for the end of Prohibition, and 55,448 vote against.
1921, February 23	The Government Liquor Act gives control over the sale, distribution, and consumption of alcohol to the provinces.
1921, June 15	The first government liquor stores appear in Victoria and Vancouver.
1922, January 1	All traffic in British Columbia switches from the left side of the road to the right.
1923, January 30	The third version of the Goldstream Hotel is destroyed by fire.
1923	Coal production peaks in Nanaimo; most of the world's shipping still uses coal for fuel.
1925, March	The first beer parlour licences are granted to BC hotel beer parlours.
1925	Joe Charlebois opens the Bowser Hotel in that community.

1926	In Cassidy, Napoleon Manca converts his general store into the Cassidy Hotel and Beer Parlour to take advantage of the new beer parlour licences.
1927	The Island Highway is widened and improved.
1927, May	The Strathcona Lodge (Hotel) becomes a private school for girls.
1930, December 13	Mary May "Ma" Miller opens the Goldstream Inn beer parlour.
1934	A rare hurricane causes considerable damage on central Vancouver Island. Thousands of trees are blown down in the Chemainus area alone.
1936, March	The Colwood Hotel is demolished to make way for the new Colwood Inn.
1938, May 1	Jim Sturgeon hires Jack Thompson to build the Fanny Bay Inn.
1941	Mike the bartending dog of the Bowser Hotel is hit by an automobile and killed.
1946, June 23	An earthquake strikes Vancouver Island at 10:14 AM, lasting thirty seconds and measuring 7.3 on the Richter scale. It causes a large number of chimneys to fall and the deaths of a handful of people.
1947, June 24	The City of Campbell River is incorporated.
1953	The CPR discontinues passenger service to the Alberni Valley.
1955, May 22	The Nelson Hotel in Union Bay is destroyed by fire.
1958, April	Ripple Rock, a maritime hazard near Campbell River, is blown up in the largest non-nuclear explosion to date, in which 1,400 tons of dynamite was used. The event is televised across Canada.
1959	The Crescent Hotel in Nanaimo is demolished.
1963, January 19	The Willows Hotel in Campbell River is destroyed by fire; four people are killed and eight others injured.

1967, October 28	The twin cities of Alberni and Port Alberni amalgamate to form Port Alberni, with a combined population of 18,538.
1968, January 2	The Riverside Hotel in Courtenay is destroyed by fire.
1969, May 3	The Bowser Hotel is destroyed by fire.
1969	The Qualicum Beach Inn closes when the owners retire.
1973, January 19	The Elk Hotel in Comox is destroyed by fire.
1974, September 2	The Forbes Landing Hotel is destroyed by fire.
1979	Via Rail, a Crown corporation, assumes operational control for passenger service between Victoria and Courtenay along the E&N.
1990, September 13–14	The Tzouhalem Hotel in Duncan is demolished.
1998	CPR sells the east–west corridor of the E&N between Parksville and Port Alberni to Rail America.
2011, February 28	The historic Lorne Hotel, operating as a pub, is destroyed by an early morning fire.
2011, March	All passenger service is discontinued on the E&N due to the poor condition of key bridges and sections of track.
2012, March	The Crossroads Bar and Grill, renamed from the Colwood Inn, closes and is moved off site to make way for a new development.
2012, May	The Arlington Hotel in Port Alberni changes hands, and with the new owner comes a new name, the Blue Marlin Inn.
2013	The Somass Hotel closes and is demolished.
2016, July	The Cassidy Inn, vacant since 2012, is destroyed by fire.
2017, June 27	The Quinsam Hotel in Campbell River is destroyed by fire.
2017, October 22	The Cambie Esquimalt Pub closes.

2017, December	The Crossroads Bar and Grill building (formerly the Colwood Inn) is demolished.
2018, August	Glen Mofford gets closer to completing his manuscript.

APPENDIX B

Select Biographies

Beech, Fredrick (Fred) Charles (chapter 3) Beech was one of hundreds of miners employed at the copper mines in the early 1900s on Mount Sicker in the North Cowichan District. Unfortunately, he is remembered for his murder of his friend and owner of the Brenton Hotel at Mount Sicker, Joe Bibeau, and for the attempted murder of Mrs. Campbell and her love interest, Mr. Hardy. Beech came to an unhappy end when he was confronted by police constables and took his own life.

Bland, James William and Elizabeth (chapter 1) Owners of the Halfway House, later known as the Esquimalt Inn, from 1860 to 1888. They built their home and tavern on their large property in Esquimalt and sunk wells to draw water to brew their own beer. They paid into a scheme to introduce camels as pack animals to be used in the Cariboo gold rush and operated their business successfully for twenty-eight years before retiring. Little did they realize that the business they began in 1860 would become the oldest privately owned business in Esquimalt, lasting until 2017.

Campbell, Daniel (chapter 1) Proprietor of the Colwood Hotel from 1913 to 1919, Campbell is perhaps better known as the person who shot and killed popular labour leader and draft evader Albert "Ginger" Goodwin near Cumberland in 1918.

Cliffe, Samuel Jackson (chapter 8) Long-time proprietor of the Lorne Hotel and a Comox pioneer. Cliffe arrived on Vancouver Island in November 1862 with his brother, Robert Cliffe, from England. He prospected for a few years, first in the Cariboo during the gold rush there and then in the Cumberland area, where he found a coal seam and bought into the Union Coal Company. Cliffe is best remembered as the jovial story-telling owner and bartender at the popular Lorne Hotel in Comox from 1883 until his death in 1908. Sam and his wife, Florence, had fifteen children, ten of whom lived into adulthood.

Dickie, Charles Herbert (chapter 3) Proprietor of the Alderlea Hotel in Duncan. Dickie was a large, strong, John Wayne type who did not suffer fools gladly. He had a checkered career, first working for the E&N until he was fired for threatening to stuff an engineer into the firebox. His next job as the owner of the Alderlea Hotel was better suited to his talents. He worked and played in the hotel bar and took delight in tossing any troublemakers out onto the street. By cleaning out the riff-raff, he made the Alderlea Hotel bar a money-maker. Dickie, ever searching for a challenge, ran for office as the local MLA, and won. He proved to be an astute politician and later ran successfully as a Member of Parliament representing the Cowichan District.

Dunsmuir, James Son of coal baron Robert Dunsmuir and president of the E&N Railway from 1889 to 1905. James and his brother Alex inherited the mighty Dunsmuir empire based on coal as well as the E&N, which their father, Robert, had built. James was more ruthless than his father when it came to labour relations.

Dunsmuir, Robert Coal-baron owner of the E&N Railway. Robert Dunsmuir was an independent coal miner who ascended the social ladder based on hard work and knowing how to play the capitalist game. He gained great wealth on the way up, and once there, appeared to have gained more power and dollars than sense—especially when it came to labour relations.

English, Jim "The Bishop" (chapter 9) Long-time owner of the Quinsam Hotel (1923–1959) in Campbellton, later part of Campbell River. The colourful English had previously owned and operated a taxi and bootlegging service in town, and before that, he was a "powder monkey," the person responsible for handling dynamite for a local company until an unfortunate accident blew some of his fingers off. Why was he known as the Bishop? You'll have to read the book.

McMurtrie, Andrew J. (chapter 4) Mayor of Wellington and owner of the Abbotsford Hotel, which he moved by E&N train to Ladysmith.

Mike the dog (chapter 7) The only non-human profiled is certainly worthy of mention. A sheepdog–terrier cross, Mike the dog worked the bar at the Bowser Hotel for eight years. He would carry beer over to a customer's table and collect the payment in his teeth, then go to the till, deposit the payment, and bring back any change. He also brought a bottle opener to the table. Mike the dog became quite a celebrity, making it into *Life* magazine and the *New York Sun*.

Miller, May Mary "Ma" (chapter 1) A colourful and long-time hotelier, Ma Miller was the proprietor and owner of the Goldstream Hotel (later called the Colwood Hotel and then the Goldstream Inn) from 1910 to 1946. Widowed at an early age, she proved to be a smart business woman at a time when there were few female proprietors.

Money, Brigadier General Noel Ernest, CMG, DSO, TD (chapter 7)   The distinguished owner and proprietor, along with his wife, Maud Boileau Money, of the Qualicum Beach Hotel and the adjoining golf course, from 1912 to 1940, with a few breaks to lead soldiers into battle at Palestine during the Great War.

Quocksister, Herman (chapter 9)   Mr. Quocksister was a guest at the Willows Hotel in Campbell River on the fateful day when the last incarnation of the hotel was destroyed by fire. Quocksister registered as a guest early in the morning of January 19, 1963. As he was heading to his room and to bed on the second floor, he passed one of the rooms and noticed dark smoke billowing out from under the door. Quocksister immediately turned and ran back down the hall and down the stairs to alert the night clerk, then rushed throughout the hotel and knocked loudly on each door to warn the other guests that a fire had broken out in the hotel and to get out as soon as possible. Despite the increasing heat and smoke, he continued to warn hotel guests of the fire danger until he was forced to run for his own life from the encroaching flames. Lives were saved that morning due to Quocksister's quick thinking and actions.

Thulin, Charles (chapter 9)   A stalwart and determined hotelman who emigrated from Sweden and with his brother Fred and wife, Mary, to Lund on the Sunshine Coast and Campbell River on Vancouver Island. His Willows Hotel in Campbell River lasted from 1904 to 1963. His offspring later operated a neighbourhood pub in the Campbell River area in the 1980s and '90s.

Wagner, Henry (chapter 7)   A desperado who once rode with the infamous Hole-in-the-Wall Gang in Wyoming. Wagner found his way up to British Columbia and, using a hideout on Lasqueti Island as a base, carried out a number of robberies along the central east coast of Vancouver Island from 1911 to 1913 with accomplice Bill Julian. He met his Waterloo at Union Bay when attempting to rob the store there. The two robbers got into a gun battle with several police constables. Wagner killed one of them, Constable Westaway, before he was apprehended by the other. He was convicted and sentenced to hang. Wagner attempted to cheat the gallows with two unsuccessful suicide attempts. His execution was carried out on the morning of August 28, 1913.

BIBLIOGRAPHY

Barman, Jean. *The West Beyond the West: A History of British Columbia*. Third Edition. Toronto: University of Toronto Press, 2007.

Barr, Jennifer Nell. *Cumberland Heritage: A Selected History of People, Buildings, Institutions and Sites, 1888–1950*. Cumberland, BC: Corporation of the Village of Cumberland, 1997.

Beautiful Rocks—A History of the Highland District. Victoria, BC: Highlands Historical Society, 2008.

Bosher, J.F. *Imperial Vancouver Island: Who Was Who 1850–1950*. Bloomington, Indiana: Xlibris Corporation, 2010.

Bowen, Lynne. *Boss Whistle: The Coal Miners of Vancouver Island Remember*. Nanaimo, BC: Nanaimo and District Museum Society and Rocky Mountain Books, 2002.

Brown, Ron. *The Train Doesn't Stop Here Anymore: An Illustrated History of Railway Stations in Canada*. Third Edition. Toronto: Dundurn Press, 2008.

Caldwell, Michael. *The Book of Great Canadian Watering Holes*. West Vancouver, BC: Creative Classic Publications, 2004.

Campbell, Robert A. *Demon Rum or Easy Money: Government Control of Liquor in British Columbia from Prohibition to Privatization*. Ottawa: Carleton University Press, 1991.

Clark, Cecil. *Tales of the British Columbia Provincial Police*. Sidney, BC: Gray's Publishing, 1971.

Dickinson, Christine, Deborah Griffiths, Judy Hagen, and Catherine Siba. *Watershed Moments: A Pictorial History of Courtenay and District*. Madeira Park, BC: Harbour Publishing, 2015.

Duffus, Maureen, ed. *Beyond the Blue Bridge: Stories from Esquimalt*. Esquimalt: Silver Threads Writers Group, 1990.

Duffus, Maureen. *Craigflower Country: A History of View Royal, 1850–1950*. Victoria, BC: Town and Gown Press, 2011.

Duffus, Maureen. *Old Langford: An Illustrated History, 1850–1950*. Victoria, BC: Town and Gown Press, 2003

Elliott, Gordon R., ed. *Memories of the Chemainus Valley: A History of People*. Compiled by Lillian Gustafson. Chemainus, BC: Chemainus Historical Society, 1978.

Elliott, Gordon R., and Ian Kennedy. *The Pick of the Neighbourhood Pubs: A Guided Tour in British Columbia*. Surrey, BC: Heritage House Publishing, 1986.

Fleming, R.B. *Peter Gzowski: A Biography*. Toronto: Dundurn Press, 2010.

Goodacre, Richard. *Dunsmuir's Dream: Ladysmith, the First Fifty Years*. Victoria, BC: Porcepic Books, 1991.

Gough, Barry. *Britannia's Navy on the West Coast of North America, 1812–1914*. Victoria, BC: Heritage House Books, 2016.

Grant, Peter. *Wish You Were Here: Life on Vancouver Island in Historical Photographs*. Victoria, BC: TouchWood Editions, 2002.

Hagen, Judy. *Courtenay: 100 Years of History, 1915–2015*. Courtenay, BC: The Courtenay and District Museum and Historical Society, 2015.

Hagen, Judy, and Catherine Siba. *Comox Valley Memories: Reminiscences of Early Life in Central Vancouver Island*. Courtenay, BC: Courtenay and District Museum and Historical Society, 1993.

Hamilton, Douglas L. *Sobering Dilemma: A History of Prohibition in British Columbia*. Vancouver, BC: Ronsdale Press, 2004.

Henry, Tom. *Small City in a Big Valley: The Story of Duncan*. Madeira Park, BC: Harbour Publishing, 1999.

Heron, Craig. *Booze: A Distilled History*. Toronto: Between the Lines, 2003.

Hind, Patrick O. *Cumberland Collieries' Railway, Vancouver Island, BC, 1888–1960*. Cumberland, BC: Cumberland Museum and Archives, 2013.

Hinde, John R. *When Coal Was King: Ladysmith and the Coal-Mining Industry on Vancouver Island*. Vancouver, BC: UBC Press, 2003.

Isenor, D.E., E.G. Stephens, and D.E. Watson. *Edge of Discovery: A History of the Campbell River District*. Campbell River, BC: Ptarmigan Press, 1989.

Isenor, D.E., E.G. Stephens, and D.E. Watson. *One Hundred Spirited Years: A History of Cumberland*. Campbell River, BC: Ptarmigan Press, 1988.

Johnson, Patricia M. *Nanaimo*. Nanaimo: Trendex Publications and Western Heritage, 1974.

Kluckner, Michael. *Vanishing British Columbia*. Vancouver, BC: UBC Press, 2005.

Lantzville Historical Society. *Lantzville: The First One Hundred Years*. Compiled and edited by Lynn Reeve. Lantzville, BC: Lantzville Historical Society, 2007.

Levitz, Rita, and Leah Willott. *Images and Voices of Lighthouse Country: A Pictorial History of Deep Bay, Bowser, Qualicum Bay and Horne Lake*. Bowser, BC: Merchants of Bowser, 1997.

Luxton, Donald, ed. *Building the West: The Early Architects of British Columbia*. Revised Second Edition. Vancouver, BC: Talonbooks, 2007.

Macham, Robert S. *Chemainus: A Town Built Upon Lumber, 1862–2012*. Nanaimo, BC: Misery Creek Bookworks, 2013.

Mackie, Richard Somerset. *The Wilderness Profound: Victorian Life on the Gulf of Georgia*. Second Edition. Victoria, BC: Sono Nis Press, 2002.

MacLachlan, Donald F. *The Esquimalt & Nanaimo Railway: The Dunsmuir Years: 1884–1905*. Victoria, BC: British Columbia Railway Association, 1986.

Mayo, Joan. *Paldi Remembered: 50 Years in the Life of a Vancouver Island Logging Town*. Duncan, BC: Paldi History Committee, 1997.

McKillop, A.B. *Pierre Berton: A Biography*. Toronto: McClelland & Stewart, 2008.

Mofford, Glen A. *Aqua Vitae: A History of the Saloons and Hotel Bars of Victoria, 1851–1917*. Victoria, BC: TouchWood Editions, 2016.

Moyes, Robert. *Island Pubbing II: A Guide to Pubs on Vancouver Island and the Gulf Islands*. Victoria, BC: Orca Book Publishers, 1991.

Norcross, E. Blanche, ed. *Nanaimo Retrospective: The First Century.* Nanaimo, BC: Nanaimo Historical Society, 1979.

Ormsby, Margaret. *British Columbia: A History.* Toronto: Macmillan, 1958.

Paterson, T.W. *Cowichan Chronicles,* vol. 1. Duncan, BC: Firgrove Publishing, 2001.

Paterson, T.W., and Garnet Basque. *Ghost Towns and Mining Camps of Vancouver Island.* Surrey, BC: Heritage House; second printing, 2006.

Paterson, T.W. "Williams: One of Cowichan's First Tour Operators." *The Cowichan Valley Citizen,* February 6, 2015.

Peterson, Jan. *Black Diamond City, Nanaimo—The Victorian Era.* Surrey, BC: Heritage House, 2002.

Peterson, Jan. *Journeys Down the Alberni Canal to Barkley Sound.* Lantzville, BC: Oolichan Books, 1999.

Peterson, Jan. *Kilts on the Coast: The Scots Who Built BC.* Victoria, BC: Heritage House, 2012.

Peterson, Jan. *Mark Bate: Nanaimo's First Mayor.* Victoria, BC: Heritage House, 2017.

Peterson, Jan. *The Albernis, 1860–1922.* Lantzville, BC: Oolichan Books, 1992.

Peterson, Jan. *Twin Cities, Alberni—Port Alberni.* Lantzville, BC: Oolichan Books, 1994.

Ramsey, Bruce, and Ormond Turner. *Inn-Side British Columbia by Automobile Magazine.* Co-sponsored by Standard Oil Company of British Columbia and the British Columbia Hotels Association. Vancouver, BC: Turner Publication, 1963.

Reksten, Terry. *The Illustrated History of British Columbia.* Vancouver and Toronto: Douglas & McIntyre, 2001.

Stonebanks, Roger. *Fighting for Dignity: The Ginger Goodwin Story.* St. John's, Newfoundland: Canadian Committee on Labour History, 2004.

Taylor, Jeanette. *River City: A History of Campbell River and the Discovery Islands.* Madeira Park, BC: Harbour Publishing, 1999.

Turner, Robert D. and Donald F. MacLachlan. *The Canadian Pacific's Esquimalt & Nanaimo Railway: The Steam Years, 1905–1949*. Winlaw, BC: Sono Nis Press, 2012.

Turner, Robert D., and Donald. F. MacLachlan. *Vancouver Island's Esquimalt & Nanaimo Railway: The Canadian Pacific, Via Rail & Shortline Years, 1949–2013*. Winlaw, BC: Sono Nis Press, 2013.

Tyrrell, Bob, and Boyd Corrigan. *Island Pubbing: A Guide to Pubs on Vancouver Island and the Gulf Islands*. Nanaimo, BC: Phantom Press, 1984.

White, Elwood, and David Wilkie. *Shays on the Switchbacks: A History of the Narrow Gauge Lenora, Mt. Sicker Railway*. Revised Edition. Victoria, BC: British Columbia Railroad Association, 1973.

Wylie, Brad. *Qualicum Beach: A History of Vancouver Island's Best Secrets*. Self-published, 1990.

Zuehlke, Mark. *Scoundrels, Dreamers & Second Sons: British Remittance Men in the Canadian West*. Madeira Park, BC: Harbour Publishing, 2016.

ENDNOTES

INTRODUCTION

[1] A.B. McKillop, *Pierre Berton: A Biography* (Toronto: McClelland & Stewart, 2008), 473–74.

[2] R.B. Fleming, *Peter Gzowski: A Biography* (Toronto: Dundurn Press, 2010), 152.

[3] Robert S. Macham, *Chemainus: A Town Built Upon Lumber, 1862–2012* (Nanaimo: Misery Creek Bookworks, 2013), 9.

[4] Ibid., 11.

CHAPTER 1: ESQUIMALT DISTRICT

[1] Township of Esquimalt, *History of Esquimalt*, https://www.esquimalt.ca/sites/default/files/docs/business-development/final_history_of_esquimalt_formatted.pdf.

[2] Richard Goodacre, *Dunsmuir's Dream: Ladysmith, the First Fifty Years* (Victoria: Porcepic Books, 1991), 17.

[3] Donald F. MacLachlan, *The Esquimalt & Nanaimo Railway: The Dunsmuir Years: 1884–1905* (Victoria: British Columbia Railroad Association), 17.

[4] Victoria West, which included the original Songhees village, was part of Esquimalt District until 1890.

[5] MacLachlan, *The Esquimalt & Nanaimo Railway*, 42.

[6] The Halfway House went through many name changes over the years: the Trentham Hotel, the Esquimalt Inn, and finally the Cambie at Esquimalt Pub.

7 Sherri Robinson, "Victoria Families: The Bland Family of Esquimalt," accessed August 16, 2018, http://www.maureenduffus.com/families/bland-family.html. Sherri Robinson is the great-great-granddaughter of James and Elizabeth Bland, owners of the Halfway House.

8 Sherri Robinson, "The Halfway House," in *Beyond the Blue Bridge: Stories from Esquimalt*, ed. Maureen Duffus (Esquimalt: Silver Threads Writers Group, 1990), 143.

9 Robinson, "The Halfway House," 143.

10 *Daily British Colonist*, April 15, 1862, 3. The newspaper was called the *Daily British Colonist* until January 1, 1887, when the word "British" was dropped. For simplicity, *Daily Colonist* is used throughout this book.

11 Ibid.

12 *Daily British Colonist*, April 23, 1862, 3.

13 *Daily British Colonist*, July 11, 1877, 3.

14 Sherri Robinson, *Esquimalt Centennial, 1912–2012* (City of Esquimalt), 2012, 73. Ms. Robinson is the great-great-granddaughter of William and Elizabeth Bland.

15 *Daily Colonist*, November 17, 1891, 8.

16 *Daily Colonist*, November 19, 1891, 5.

17 You can read one side of the story in Barbara McLintock's book, *Smoke Free* (Vancouver: Granville Island Publishing, 2004), 121–23.

18 Information supplied by Pam Gaudio in *Beautiful Rocks—A History of the Highland District* (Victoria: Highlands Historical Society, 2008), 68.

19 *Daily British Colonist*, July 4, 1864, 3.

20 Maureen Duffus, *Craigflower Country: A History of View Royal, 1850–1950* (Victoria: Town and Gown Press, 2011), 44.

21 *Daily Colonist*, August 6, 1872, 2.

22 *Daily Colonist*, July 21, 1877, 3.

23 *Daily Colonist*, July 12, 1878, 3.

24 *Daily Colonist*, February 14, 1879, 2.

25 Read about the life of Robert Kerr (Ker) in historian John Adams's book *The Ker Family of Victoria, 1859–1976: Pioneer Industrialists in Western Canada* (Vancouver: Holte Publishing, 2007).

26 British Columbia Vital Statistics, Marriage Registry #1879-09-002469.

27 Ibid., Death Registry #1884-09-003858.

28 *Daily Colonist*, December 20, 1885, 3.

29 Duffus, *Craigflower Country*, 47.

30 *Daily Colonist and Morning Chronicle*, January 8, 1867, 3.

31 Duffus, *Craigflower Country*, 47.

32 Ibid.

33 *Daily Colonist*, June 16, 1898, 6.

34 MacLachlan, *The Esquimalt & Nanaimo Railway*, 112.

35 "E&N Freight Train Wrecked," *Daily Colonist*, November 5, 1905, 1.

36 *Daily Colonist*, June 3, 1911, 6.

37 *Daily Colonist*, September 24, 1913, 6.

38 Duffus, *Craigflower Country,* 47.

39 Glen A. Mofford, *Aqua Vitae: A History of the Saloons and Hotel Bars of Victoria, 1851–1917* (Victoria: TouchWood Editions, 2016), 33.

40 *Daily Colonist*, December 4, 1894, 1.

41 *Daily Colonist*, December 13, 1895, 6.

42 *Daily Colonist*, January 5, 1896, 6.

43 *Daily Colonist*, September 11, 1902, 5.

44 "Row at Colwood Hotel—Soldier Shot in Leg by Proprietor," *Daily Colonist*, August 9, 1904, 5.

45 Roger Stonebanks, *Fighting for Dignity: The Ginger Goodwin Story* (St. John's: Canadian Committee on Labour History, 2004), 97–98.

46 *Daily Colonist*, December 17, 1915, 3.

47 Stonebanks, *Fighting for Dignity*, 1.

48 Ibid., 102. Much more can be read regarding Campbell and Goodwin in chapter 8.

49 Ibid.

50 *Daily Colonist*, March 5, 1936, 1.

51 Kendra Wong, "Old Colwood Pub Being Torn Down," *Goldstream Gazette*, December 21, 2017, https://www.goldstreamgazette.com/news /old-colwood-pub-being-torn-down/.

52 *Daily Colonist*, October 24, 1863, 3.

53 *Daily Colonist*, April 8, 1864, 3.

54 *Daily Colonist*, March 18, 1865, 3.

55 *Daily Colonist*, September 19, 1868, 3.

56 *Daily Colonist*, October 21, 1870, 2.

57 *Daily Colonist*, July 30, 1880, 3.

58 *Daily Colonist*, February 5, 1887, 3.

59 Donald Luxton, ed., *Building the West: The Early Architects of British Columbia*, rev. 2nd ed. (Vancouver: Talonbooks, 2007), 122.

60 MacLachlan, *The Esquimalt & Nanaimo Railway*, 67.

61 Maureen Duffus, *Old Langford: An Illustrated History, 1850–1950* (Victoria: Town and Gown Press, 2003), 118.

62 Ibid., 118.

63 *Daily Colonist*, April 7, 1910, 6.

64 *Daily Colonist*, July 7, 1915, 5.

65 "Crushed to Death in Motor Accident," *Daily Colonist*, July 7, 1915, 5.

66 *Daily Colonist*, August 18, 1920, 7.

CHAPTER 2: SHAWNIGAN LAKE TO COWICHAN BAY

1 MacLachlan, *The Esquimalt & Nanaimo Railway*, 26.

2 Ibid., 69.

3 Ibid., 57.

4 Diana Pedersen, *An Angler's Paradise: Sportfishing and Settler Society on Vancouver Island, 1860s–1920s* (blog), https://anglersparadise.wordpress.com /author/anglersparadise/.

5 *Daily Colonist*, March 22, 1883, 2.

6 *Daily Colonist*, February 12, 1884, 3.

7   *Daily Colonist*, July 18, 1885, 3.

8   *Daily Colonist*, December 22, 1886, 3.

9   *Daily Colonist*, April 5, 1887, 1.

10 *Daily Colonist*, April 30, 1887, 2.

11 *Daily Colonist*, January 4, 1891, 1.

12 *Daily Colonist*, October 29, 1891, 2.

13 Pedersen, *An Angler's Paradise,* "The Morton House at Shawnigan Lake", see: https://anglersparadise.wordpress.com/2017/02/03/the-morton-house-at-shawnigan-lake/#more-275

14 MacLachlan, *The Esquimalt & Nanaimo Railway*, 67–69.

15 "Burned to the Ground—Koenig's Hotel at Shawnigan Lake Was Destroyed by Fire Yesterday," *Daily Colonist*, December 17, 1901, 5.

16 *Crofton Gazette and Cowichan News*, June 5, 1902, 7.

17 "Late George Koenig—No Evidence He Committed Suicide," *Daily Colonist*, June 10, 1902, 2.

18 *Cranbrook Herald*, January 2, 1913, 5.

19 *Daily Colonist*, June 23, 1915, 10.

20 Jim Wolf, "Samuel Maclure," in Luxton, *Building the West*, 152.

21 Lori Treloar, *The Strathcona Hotel*, http://shawniganlakemuseum.com/resources/Documents/E%20%26%20N%20.pdf.

22 *Daily Colonist*, May 15, 1900, 5.

23 Lori Treloar, The Strathcona Hotel.

24 *Daily Colonist*, November 21, 1903, 5.

25 *Daily Colonist*, July 27, 1904, 6.

26 Ron Brown, *The Train Doesn't Stop Here Anymore: An Illustrated History of Railway Stations in Canada*, 3rd ed. (Toronto: Dundurn Press, 2008), 120.

27 *Daily Colonist*, March 14, 1915, 8.

28 Read more about the details of this tragic event in the *Daily Colonist*, September 1, 1926, 1.

29 See Cowichan Valley Regional District, *Cobble Hill Village Plan—Schedule A, Appendix C: Official Community Plan* no. 3510, http://cvrd.bc.ca /DocumentCenter/Home/View/7508.

30 *Daily Colonist,* April 20, 1911, 17.

31 *Daily Colonist,* January 22, 1893, 2.

32 *Daily Colonist,* February 2, 1908, 2.

33 *Daily Colonist,* April 18, 1917, 12.

34 Government of British Columbia, *1925 Annual Report Liquor Control Board* (Victoria: Queen's Printer, 1925), J10.

35 Unless supplied with a valid liquor permit, Indigenous people were not permitted to buy beer or spirits until the law was changed in 1965.

36 *Daily Colonist,* January 7, 1933, 1–2.

37 Ibid., 2.

38 *Daily Colonist,* January 10, 1933, 6.

39 Known as the Bonner Block in Cobble Hill.

40 *Daily Colonist,* December 2, 1942, 5.

41 More information about Samuel Harris and the early years at Cowichan Bay can be found in T.W. Paterson's informative *Cowichan Chronicles,* vol. 1 (Duncan, BC: Firgrove Publishing, 2001).

42 *Daily Colonist,* May 19, 1908, 11.

43 *Daily Colonist,* June 27, 1908, 16.

44 The hotel was built on a hill overlooking Cowichan Bay. Today, an apartment building occupies the site near the corner of Cowichan Bay Road and Wilmot Road.

45 *Daily Colonist,* July 2, 1916, 7.

46 *Daily Colonist,* May 24, 1933, 6.

47 "Fire Destroys Part of Hotel—Buena Vista Annex Total Loss," *Daily Colonist,* November 22, 1939, 3.

48 *Daily Colonist,* May 10, 1946, 11.

49 John Wagner, *Cowichan Bay from 1850 to Now* (blog), http://crabbyoldbugger .com/writing/hotel%20fires.html. Wagner's blog also includes more about the Buena Vista Hotel and a history of Cowichan Bay.

[1] Elliott, Gordon R., ed. *Memories of the Chemainus Valley: A History of People.* Compiled by Lillian Gustafson. (Chemainus, BC: Chemainus Historical Society, 1978).

[2] Thomas Henry, *Small City in a Big Valley: The Story of Duncan* (Madeira Park, BC: Harbour Publishing, 1999), 27.

[3] Henry, *Small City in a Big Valley*, 27.

[4] *Henderson's BC Gazetteer and Directory for 1900–1901*, 254.

[5] Henry, *Small City in a Big Valley*, 33.

[6] Paterson, *Cowichan Chronicles*, 76.

[7] Ibid.

[8] Ibid., 77.

[9] Henry, *Small City in a Big Valley*, 33.

[10] *Daily Colonist*, February 19, 1893, 2.

[11] *Daily Colonist*, March 5, 1893, 2.

[12] *Crofton Gazette and Cowichan News*, March 6, 1902, 6. After leaving the Alderlea, Pitt purchased the Duncan Emporium from Harry Smith, who was responsible for starting the first newspaper in Duncan, the *Duncan Enterprise* (1900–1905), which was eventually bought out and renamed the *Cowichan Leader*.

[13] *Cowichan Leader*, January 8, 1904.

[14] *Duncan Leader*, April 13, 1913. Also mentioned by John King on Facebook.

[15] *Duncan Enterprise*, January 14, 1914, 2; *Daily Building Record* (Vancouver), August 20, 1913, 1.

[16] Frank Price's son, Fred, chats about his father's hotel in an informative video, https://www.youtube.com/watch?v=jNzQKob1oms#t=12.

[17] "Quamichan," Wikipedia, last modified June 12, 2016, https://en.wikipedia.org /wiki/Quamichan.

[18] The Price brothers also built the Tzouhalem Hotel in Duncan in 1901 and the Lakeside Hotel at Lake Cowichan in 1891. A message sent to the author from Keith Price, the grandson of Frank and Edith Price, set the record straight about the Price family and the three historic hotels.

[19] *Daily Colonist*, November 3, 1891, 8.

20 *Daily Colonist*, December 6, 1893, 2.

21 *Daily Colonist*, September 23, 1900, 9.

22 *Crofton Gazette and Cowichan News*, March 6, 1902, 6.

23 *Vancouver Daily World*, March 3, 1902, 6.

24 *Crofton Gazette and Cowichan News*, June 12, 1902, 3.

25 *Crofton Gazette and Cowichan News*, July 10, 1902, 6.

26 *Daily Colonist*, October 23, 1902, 1.

27 "Liquor Selling Case—Duncan," *Daily Colonist*, November 8, 1925, 7.

28 Paterson, *Cowichan Chronicles*, 10.

29 Mark Zuehlke, *Scoundrels, Dreamers & Second Sons: British Remittance Men in the Canadian West* (Madeira Park, BC: Harbour Publishing, 2016), 28.

30 Fred Price chats about the Tzouhalem Hotel in a video, https://www.youtube.com/watch?v=jNzQK0b1oMs#t=12.

31 I received this information from one of Percy Odgers's great-grandsons.

32 Lexi Bainas, *The Citizen*, August 24, 2011.

33 The story of Paldi and its remarkable founder, Mayo Singh, is told in Joan Mayo, *Paldi Remembered: 50 Years in the Life of a Vancouver Island Logging Town* (Paldi: Paldi History Committee, 1997).

34 "Up the Line of the E&N," *Daily Colonist*, September 23, 1900, 9–10, provides an excellent description of the Mount Sicker copper operation during the early years of its existence.

35 To learn more about Harry Smith, Mount Sicker, and the early years of Duncan, see https://www.youtube.com/watch?v=jNzQK0b1oMs#t=12.

36 *Daily Colonist*, April 16, 1901, 8.

37 Ibid.

38 Bibeau's name is spelled in various ways in historical sources. There are also a number of variations to the tragic story of Fred Beech and how his jealous rage ended in murder and suicide, the best being from the *Daily Colonist*, August 22, 1905, 3. Elwood White and David Wilkie provide good background to the history of Mount Sicker mines and the Beech shooting in their book *Shays on the Switchback: A History of the Narrow Gauge Lenora, Mt. Sicker Railway*, rev. ed. (Victoria: British Columbia Railroad Association, 1973).

[39] Another account claims that Beech was forty-two at the time of these events.

[40] White and Wilkie, *Shays on the Switchbacks*, 26.

[41] Ibid.

[42] *Daily Colonist*, May 1, 1908, 16.

[43] Jack the Younger, "The Pinsons," in *Memories of the Chemainus Valley*, 129.

CHAPTER 4: CHEMAINUS TO LADYSMITH

[1] *Daily Colonist*, August 29, 1890, 3.

[2] Macham, *Chemainus*, 1.

[3] Ibid., 5.

[4] Ibid., 6.

[5] Richard Goodacre, *Dunsmuir's Dream: Ladysmith, the First Fifty Years* (Victoria: Porcepic Books, 1991), 29.

[6] *Daily Colonist*, September 23, 1900, 10.

[7] For a history of the area and the two major hotels, see Elliott, *Memories of the Chemainus Valley: A History of People*. Compiled by Lillian Gustafson. (Chemainus, BC: Chemainus Historical Society, 1978).

[8] *Daily Colonist*, September 23, 1900, 10.

[9] Elliott, *Memories of the Chemainus Valley*, 197.

[10] *Daily Colonist*, October 6, 1893, 2.

[11] Elliott, *Memories of the Chemainus Valley*, 195.

[12] *Daily Colonist*, October 22, 1905, 15.

[13] Gwen Cash, "Lumber and the Inn," *Daily Colonist* (Sunday supplement), March 25, 1956, 13.

[14] *Daily Colonist*, September 13, 1923, 14.

[15] From a letter that Arthur E. Collyer (mistakenly spelled "Callyton") wrote on June 24, 1912, while proprietor of the Horseshoe Bay Hotel, http://hpcanpub .mcmaster.ca/hpcanpub/media/letter-arthur-e-callyton-pauline-johnson-24 -june-1912; Jack Howe, "1892, Horseshoe Bay Hotel," in Elliott, *Memories of the Chemainus Valley*, 190–91.

16 Catherine Collyer McNally, in Elliott's *Memories of the Chemainus Valley*, 251–53.

17 *Daily Colonist*, April 19, 1961, 11.

18 See "The Little Town That Did," https://muraltown.com/background/history.

19 *Cumberland News*, March 11, 1907, 1.

20 "William Smithe," Wikipedia, last modified June 26, 2018, https://en.wikipedia .org/wiki/William_Smithe.

21 *Daily Colonist*, February 17, 1935, 22.

22 Tom Guilbride, in Elliott's *Memories of the Chemainus Valley*, 278.

23 The name would change again from the Green Lantern Hotel to the Green Lantern Inn many years later.

24 Mary Crucil, "The Crucil Story," in Elliott's *Memories of the Chemainus Valley*, 324–28.

25 Ibid.

26 John R. Hinde, *When Coal Was King: Ladysmith and the Coal-Mining Industry on Vancouver Island* (Vancouver: UBC Press, 2003), 15.

27 Goodacre, *Dunsmuir's Dream*, 36.

28 Douglas L. Hamilton, *Sobering Dilemma: A History of Prohibition in British Columbia* (Vancouver: Ronsdale Press, 2004), 35.

29 *Daily Colonist*, November 4, 1893, 2.

30 *Daily Colonist*, January 14, 1898, 2.

31 *Daily Colonist*, January 12, 1899, 5.

32 *Ladysmith Leader and Wellington-Extension News*, March 1, 1902, 1.

33 *Ladysmith Daily Ledger*, October 23, 1905, 1.

34 Goodacre, *Dunsmuir's Dream*, 30.

35 *Ladysmith General Ledger*, February 23, 1905, 4.

36 *Ladysmith Standard*, July 22, 1908, 1.

37 *Daily Colonist*, October 6, 1909, 1.

38 Hinde, *When Coal Was King*, 20.

39 Goodacre, *Dunsmuir's Dream*, 31.

40 *Daily Colonist*, January 5, 1935, 6.

41 Goodacre, *Dunsmuir's Dream*, 70.

42 *Nanaimo Daily News*, January 28, 1963.

CHAPTER 5: CASSIDY TO PARKSVILLE

1 T.W. Paterson, "Ghosts of Cassidy," *Daily Colonist* (*Islander* supplement), September 3, 1967, 57.

2 *Ladysmith Standard*, June 17, 1908, 4.

3 Ibid.

4 W.Y Galey, *Daily Colonist*, December 7, 1948, 6.

5 Bob Tyrrell and Boyd Corrigan, *Island Pubbing: A Guide to Pubs on Vancouver Island and the Gulf Islands* (Nanaimo: Phantom Press, 1984), 87.

6 I received this message on my blog from a relative of Manca's: "Napoleon Manca, my grandfather, built the hotel. One of his daughters, my aunt, inherited the piano and sold it to the community of Barkerville. To my knowledge it is still there."

7 Robert Moyes, *Island Pubbing II: A Guide to Pubs on Vancouver Island and the Gulf Islands* (Victoria: Orca Book Publishers, 1991), 90.

8 Ibid., 90–91.

9 *Daily Colonist*, August 29, 1890, 3.

10 Patricia M. Johnson, "Welcome to Nanaimo," BC *Studies*, No. 24 (Winter 1974–75), 36.

11 Jan Peterson, *Mark Bate: Nanaimo's First Mayor* (Victoria: Heritage House, 2017), 135

12 *Westward Ho*, March 4, 1886, 3.

13 Nanaimo Archives: Transcripts & Recording, http://www.nanaimoarchives.ca/transcripts-recordings/historical-transcripts/lewis-william-family-history/

14 *Nanaimo Courier*, August 10, 1889, 2.

15 *Vancouver Daily World*, September 4, 1889, 1.

16 Historical sources contain various spellings of Cuffolo's surname. *The Williams Official BC Directory of 1894* mistakenly spelled his name as "Guffolo," 229.

17 *Daily Colonist*, September 29, 1894, 2.

18 *San Bernardino County Sun*, September 29, 1894, 3.

19 *Daily Colonist*, September 29, 1894, 2.

20 *Daily Colonist*, October 2, 1894, 2.

21 *Vancouver Daily World*, July 17, 1895, 8.

22 Dorothy Mindenhall and Carey Pallister, "John Teague," in Luxton, *Building the West*, 75.

23 Canada's Historic Places, http://www.historicplaces.ca/en/rep-reg/place-lieu .aspx?id=1431.

24 Jan Peterson, *Black Diamond City: Nanaimo—The Victorian Era* (Surrey, BC: Heritage House, 2002), 217.

25 T.W. Paterson, "Only the name survives of historic Fiddick's Junction," *Cowichan Valley Citizen*, July 10, 2015, https://www.cowichanvalleycitizen .com/life/only-the-name-survives-of-historic-fiddicks-junction/

26 *Daily Colonist*, August 9, 1887, 2.

27 *Daily Colonist*, November 4, 1888, 4

28 *Nanaimo Courier*, March 9, 1889, 3.

29 *Ladysmith Signal*, April 19, 1912, 1.

30 See http://www.historicplaces.ca/en/rep-reg/place-lieu.aspx?id=1431&pid=0.

31 When the E&N Railway arrived at Parksville, a handful of people, including the E&N brass, still called the community McBride (named for the premier of BC at the time). It took a few years before the E&N used the new name of Parksville for its train station.

32 *Daily Colonist*, April 17, 1913, 6.

33 For a chronology of the history of Parksville, see https://parksvillemuseum.ca /cmsb/uploads/parksville-history.pdf.

34 "Parksville Site Former Crown Grant for Settler Who Arrived in Canoe," *Daily Colonist*, December 12, 1948, 10.

35 *Daily Colonist*, October 10, 1897, 5.

36 *Daily Colonist*, December 12, 1948, 10. The amazing Ann Hirst ran the post office from 1900 until her retirement in August 1947, when she was well into her eighties. The post office was replaced when she retired.

37 Michael Kluckner, *Vanishing British Columbia* (Vancouver: UBC Press, 2005), 153.

38 Ibid.

39 For more about the Rod & Gun Pub, see Darron Kloster, "Parksville's Historic Rod & Gun Hotel Gets Makeover," *Times Colonist*, June 18, 2013, http://www .timescolonist.com/business/parksville-s-historic-rod-gun-hotel-gets-makeover -1.325397#sthash.jy2m9Vo5.dpuf.

CHAPTER 6: ALBERNI VALLEY TO GREAT CENTRAL LAKE

1   Jan Peterson, *The Albernis, 1860–1922* (Lantzville, BC: Oolichan Books, 1992), 142.

2   *Daily Colonist*, July 19, 1898, 4.

3   *Alberni Advocate*, March 22, 1912, page. 2.

4   *Daily Colonist*, July 19, 1898, 4.

5   Peterson, *The Albernis*, 96.

6   *Alberni Advocate*, September 5, 1913, 5.

7   *Alberni Advocate*, February 20, 1914, 3.

8   Jan Peterson, *Twin Cities*, 73–74.

9   As told to the author.

10 The town of New Alberni was incorporated in 1911 as Port Alberni, and Port Alberni and Alberni amalgamated in 1967.

11 Peterson, *The Albernis*, 130.

12 Jan Peterson, "Pioneer Hotel Renovated," *Twin City Times*, January 2, 1957, 12.

13 Peterson, "Pioneer Hotel Renovated," 12.

14 Dorritt MacLeod, "Port Alberni's Early Years," in *Life and Times: Memories of the 20th Century*, interviews by Gerry Fagan, ed. Diane Dobson (Port Alberni: From a series of interviews for the Echo Centre Retirement Home Newsletter, 1999), 44–45.

15 Peterson, *The Albernis*, 12.

16 Ron Newton, *Arrowsmith Star*, August 17, 1976.

17 "A Visit to the West Coast," *Daily Colonist*, June 27, 1909, 3.

[18] *Daily Colonist*, November 17, 1916, 4.

[19] Jan Peterson, *Twin Cities*, 299. Peterson mentions that Mr. Woollett felt that the Somass bar was unfairly being targeted while other local hotel bars seemed to be getting away with selling illegal beer to the customers who clamoured for it. In spite of warnings by the police to stop illegal sales, Woollett continued the practice.

[20] 1923 *Wrigley's British Columbia Directory*, 480.

[21] See "1946 Vancouver Island earthquake," Wikipedia, last modified June 21, 2018, http://en.wikipedia.org/wiki/1946_Vancouver_Island_earthquake.

[22] For more on the history of the Somass Hotel and the history of other BC hotels not covered in this book, see my blog at https://raincoasthistory.blogspot.ca/.

[23] Peterson, *The Albernis*, 215.

[24] Alberni District Museum and Historical Society, *When the Whistle Blew: The Great Central Story, 1925–1952* (Great Central Book Project Committee, 2002), 21.

[25] *Alberni Advocate*, July 4, 1913, 5.

[26] *Daily Colonist*, August 3, 1919, 20.

[27] T.W. Paterson, "Joe's Ark Provided Floating Luxury," *Harbour City Star*, March 27, 2002, B1.

[28] Peterson, *Twin Cities*, 55.

[29] *Daily Colonist*, January 12, 1965, 34.

[30] Annie Dunn, "Out Where the West Ends: The Story of Joe Drinkwater," *Daily Colonist*, June 23, 1929, 14.

[31] Robert Dunn, Jr., "Tribute to the Late Joe Drinkwater," *Daily Colonist*, January 24, 1932, 4.

[32] *When the Whistle Blew*, 22.

CHAPTER 7: QUALICUM BEACH TO UNION BAY

[1] Brad Wylie, *Qualicum Beach: A History of Vancouver Island's Best Secrets* (self-published, 1990), 28.

[2] "History of Qualicum Beach," Town of Qualicum Beach (website), https://www.qualicumbeach.com/history-of-qualicum-beach.

[3] Wylie, *Qualicum Beach*, 28.

4 Jennifer Nell Barr, "Karl Branwhite Spurgin, 1877–1936," in Luxton, *Building the West*, 392.

5 J.F. Bosher, *Imperial Vancouver Island: Who Was Who 1850–1950* (Bloomington, Indiana: Xlibris Corporation, 2010), 500–503.

6 Wylie, *Qualicum Beach*, 56.

7 Barr, "Karl Branwhite Spurgin," 392.

8 Bosher, *Imperial Vancouver Island*, 501.

9 Wylie, *Qualicum Beach*, 59–63; see also "Notable Resort is Regaining Old Flame—Qualicum Offers Delightful Headquarters for Motorists, Golfer and Fisherman—Hotel Is Crowded," *Daily Colonist*, July 27, 1921, 1. There are countless spellings of Masarati's surname in historical sources.

10 Bosher, *Imperial Vancouver Island*, 502.

11 Ibid., 501–2.

12 In 1960, Queen Elizabeth II conferred the prefix "Royal" to be used for the Royal Canadian Legion.

13 Bosher, *Imperial Vancouver Island*, 502.

14 A typical season lasted from March to the end of September each year.

15 Wylie, *Qualicum Beach*, 61.

16 *Daily Colonist*, June 1, 1941, 3.

17 Wylie, *Qualicum Beach*, 62.

18 For more information about Bowser and Lighthouse Country, see http://lighthousecountry.ca/community-services-events /lighthouse-country-history/

19 Rita Levitz and Leah Willott. *Images and Voices of Lighthouse Country: A Pictorial History of Deep Bay, Bowser, Qualicum Bay and Horne Lake*. (Bowser, BC, Merchants of Bowser, 1997), 76.

20 Ibid.,81.

21 Ibid., 82.

22 *Cumberland Islander*, June 8, 1928, 1.

23 Levitz and Willott, *Images and Voices of Lighthouse Country*, 82.

24 Beverly Keim, "Canine Barmaid." Pictures to the Editor, *Life Magazine*, June 16, 1941, Volume 10, #24.

25 "Medal May Go to Island Dog," *Daily Colonist*, December 9, 1936,1.

26 *Vancouver Province*, July 8, 1939.

27 D.E. Isenor, E.G. Stephens, and D.E. Watson, *One Hundred Spirited Years: A History of Cumberland* (Campbell River: Ptarmigan Press, 1988), 58.

28 See "Fanny Bay," Wikipedia, last modified December 20, 2017, https://en.wikipedia.org/wiki/Fanny_Bay.

29 Judy Hagen and Catherine Siba, *Comox Valley Memories: Reminiscences of Early Life in Central Vancouver Island* (Courtenay, BC: Courtenay and District Museum and Historical Society, 1993), 20.

30 Ibid., 20–21.

31 For more about the history of Union Bay, see Janette (Glover) Geidt, *Mosaic of Mining Memories* (blog), http://mining.mosaictraining.ca/janette.geidt.html.

32 Jennifer Nell Barr, *Cumberland Heritage: A Selected History of People, Buildings, Institutions and Sites, 1888–1950* (Cumberland, BC: Corporation of the Village of Cumberland, 1997), 49.

33 Ibid.

34 *Daily Colonist*, April 9, 1893, 2; *Daily Colonist*, June 18, 1893, 2.

35 *Daily Colonist*, January 26, 1897, 6.

36 "Sandwick," KnowBC.com (website), http://knowbc.com/limited/Books/Encyclopedia-of-BC/S/Sandwick.

37 Douglas Hamilton, "In Pursuit of the Flying Dutchman," http://cookingandcommunitylasqueti-island.com/in-pursuit-of-the-flying-dutchman.html.

38 Cecil Clark, *Tales of the British Columbia Provincial Police* (Sidney, BC: Gray's Publishing, 1971), 93–100.

39 Hamilton, "In Pursuit of the Flying Dutchman."

40 Clark, *Tales of the British Columbia Provincial Police*, 99.

41 *Courtenay Review*, May 15, 1913, 1.

42 *Cumberland Islander*, August 30, 1913, 1.

43 "Spectacular Blaze at Union Bay," *Cumberland Islander*, February 18, 1922, 1.

44 Ibid.

CHAPTER 8: CUMBERLAND TO COMOX

1   Barr, *Cumberland Heritage*, 11.

2   Ibid., 12.

3   Lynn Bowen, *Boss Whistle: The Coal Miners of Vancouver Island Remember* (Nanaimo, BC: Rocky Point Books and Nanaimo District Museum Society, 2002), 45.

4   Christine Dickinson et al., *Watershed Moments: A Pictorial History of Courtenay and District* (Madeira Park, BC: Harbour Publishing, 2015), 38.

5   *Courtenay Weekly News*, November 26, 1895, 5.

6   Barr, *Cumberland Heritage*, 56.

7   Barr, *Cumberland Heritage*, 93.

8   Ibid., 186–87.

9   Ibid.

10 Ibid.

11 Ibid., 56.

12 *Cumberland Islander*, June 29, 1918, 1.

13 *Cumberland Islander*, January 7, 1922, 1.

14 "Three Beer Parlours Open for Business," *Cumberland Islander,* April 10, 1925, 1.

15 *Daily Colonist*, March 11, 1925, 13.

16 *Daily Colonist*, December 3, 1925, 15.

17 *Daily Colonist,* October 15, 1927, 8.

18 Barr, *Cumberland Heritage*, 79.

19 Further information about the Waverley and its history can be found at "The Legendary Waverley Hotel," January 31, 2013, http://www.bcmusicianmag.com/the-legendary-waverley-hotel/, and Shirley Culpin, "Cumberland, BC: A Historical Treasure Trove," April 8, 2014, http://blog.hellobc.com/cumberland-bc-a-historical-treasure-trove/.

20 Richard Somerset Mackie, *The Wilderness Profound: Victorian Life on the Gulf of Georgia*, 2nd ed. (Victoria: Sono Nis Press, 2002), 234–35.

21 *Courtenay Weekly News*, November 17, 1892, 1.

22 *Courtenay Weekly News*, December 8, 1892, 1.

23 Dickinson et al., "Riverside Hotel," in *Watershed Moments*, 70.

24 Hagen, *Courtenay: One Hundred Years of History, 1915–2015*, 62.

25 *Courtenay Weekly News*, November 26, 1895, 8.

26 *Daily Colonist*, June 9, 1896, 3.

27 *Cumberland News*, December 17, 1898, 4.

28 *Cumberland News*, December 5, 1900, 8.

29 *Cumberland News*, January 1, 1902, 4.

30 *The Western Call*, March 15, 1912, 3.

31 *Cumberland News*, February 28, 1912, 1.

32 *Daily Colonist*, August 2, 1913, 6.

33 Dickinson et al., *Watershed Moments*, 70.

34 "Courtenay Has Heavy Fire Loss," *Daily Colonist*, July 22, 1916, 1.

35 *Daily Colonist*, January 3, 1968, 17.

36 Hagen and Siba, *Comox Valley Memories,* 63.

37 See "Comox Harbour History," http://comoxharbour.com/history.

38 Hagen and Siba, *Comox Valley Memories*, 28.

39 Ibid.

40 *Daily Colonist*, August 16, 1878, 2.

41 Mackie, *The Wilderness Profound*, 164.

42 Hagen and Siba, *Watershed Moments*, 14.

43 Mackie, *The Wilderness Profound*, 45.

44 Val Barager (granddaughter of Sam and Florence Cliffe) cited in Hagen and Siba, *Comox Valley Memories*, 28.

45 Mackie, *The Wilderness Profound*, 67.

46 Robert A. Campbell, *Demon Rum or Easy Money: Government Control of Liquor in British Columbia from Prohibition to Privatization* (Ottawa: Carleton University Press, 1991), 10.

47 Hagen and Siba, *Comox Valley Memories*, 28.

48 *Daily Colonist*, February 28, 1886, 3.

[49] Mackie, *The Wilderness Profound*, 166.

[50] *Courtenay Weekly News*, November 17, 1892, 1.

[51] *New Westminster Daily News*, August 23, 1906, 8.

[52] Mackie, *The Wilderness Profound*, 287.

[53] *Daily Colonist*, July 12, 1908, 1.

[54] See page 28 in Hagen and Siba's *Comox Valley Memories* for a brief description of the Lorne beer parlour.

[55] *Cumberland Islander*, April 23, 1926, 1.

[56] Hagen and Siba, *Comox Valley Memories*, 29.

[57] Ibid., 29.

[58] *Times Colonist*, February 28, 2011.

[59] Heather Diana Broere, Facebook, personal message to the author, February 28, 2011.

CHAPTER 9: CAMPBELL RIVER TO FORBES LANDING

[1] *Daily Colonist*, May 21, 1911, 35.

[2] Jeanette Taylor, *River City: A History of Campbell River and the Discovery Islands* (Madeira Park, BC: Harbour Publishing, 1999), 29.

[3] *Daily Colonist*, October 1, 1879, 3.

[4] Taylor, *River City*, 63.

[5] Ibid., 74.

[6] Ibid., 72.

[7] Ibid., 73.

[8] Ibid., 90.

[9] Ibid., 79.

[10] Ibid., 98.

[11] Ibid., 103.

[12] *Comox Argus*, August 19, 1920, 2.

[13] Taylor, *River City*, 131.

14 May Baldwin, "The Night the Willows Burned Down," *Campbell River Courier*, January 20, 1971, 14.

15 Ibid.

16 Taylor, *River City*, 179–80.

17 There are varying stories of who actually began building the Quinsam Hotel and when it was built. I have pieced together what I believe to be an accurate history of the early years of the Quinsam Hotel.

18 Taylor, *River City*, 115. English was able to buy the Quinsam and enlarge the hotel from monies he had earned selling bootleg booze during Prohibition.

19 If anybody reading this has heard an alternative story to the one here, please let me know.

20 BC *Hotelman Magazine*, July 1963, 6–7.

21 There was extensive coverage of the Quinsam Hotel fire on both major Canadian networks, CTV and CBC, followed up the next day in the newspapers and on social media.

22 The road has improved over the years, especially when Strathcona Park was established and road crews were assigned to widen and eventually pave the road west.

23 Taylor, *River City*, 93.

24 Strathcona Park is the oldest and largest provincial park in British Columbia. Della Falls, inside Strathcona Park, is the highest waterfall in Canada.

25 Go Campbell River, https://gocampbellriver.com/campbell-river-history /#forbeslanding

26 *Cumberland Islander*, April 26, 1924, 1.

27 *Wrigley's British Columbia Directory*, 1918, under "Campbell Lake" (Wrigley's Directory Limited, Vancouver, 1918), 109.

28 *Daily Colonist*, May 11, 1923, 14.

29 Taylor, *River City*, 134.

30 *News–Journal* (Mansfield, OH), July 22, 1938, 1.

31 John Parminter, *Darkness at Noon: The Bloedel Fire of 1938* (Victoria: BC Forestry Service, Research Branch, October 1994), 7. https://www.for.gov .bc.ca/hfd/pubs/docs/scv/scv871.pdf.

32 *Comox Argus*, June 8, 1939, 1.

33 *Daily Colonist*, July 8, 1941, 7.

34 "Big Tyee Salmon for Harpo Marx," *Sunshine Coast News*, September 6, 1946, 5.

35 Taylor, *River City*, 152.

36 *Daily Colonist*, June 30, 1949, 27.

37 *Kelowna Daily Courier*, July 14, 2014.

38 For more memories of Forbes Landing, see https://gohiking.ca/coastal-shores /lakes/bc-coastal-lakes-c-f/forbes-landing/.

INDEX

Note: In this index, page numbers set in *italic* type indicate an illustration.